A Handbook for Learning Support Assistants

Other titles of interest:

Early Learning Goals for Children with Special Needs
Collette Drifte

The Essential Guide for Competent Teaching Assistants
Anne Watkinson

The Essential Guide for Experienced Teaching Assistants
Anne Watkinson

Supporting Children with Behaviour Difficulties
Glenys Fox

Supporting Children with Special Educational Needs
Marian Halliwell

Supporting Language and Literacy 3–8
Suzi Clipson-Boyles

Supporting Literacy and Numeracy: A Guide for Teaching Assistants
Glenys Fox and Marian Halliwell

Supporting Special Educational Needs in Secondary School Classrooms
Jane Lovey

Teaching Assistants: Practical Strategies for Effective Classroom Support
Maggie Balshaw and Peter Farrell

A Handbook for Learning Support Assistants

Teachers and Assistants
Working Together

Revised Edition

Glenys Fox

David Fulton Publishers

This edition reprinted 2007 by Routledge
2 Park Square, Milton Park, Abingdon, Oxon, OX14 4RN
Simultaneously published in the USA and Canada
By Routledge
270 Madison Avenue, New York, NY 10016

First published in Great Britain in 1998 by David Fulton Publishers
Revised edition 2003
10 9 8 7 6 5 4 3

Note: The right of Glenys Fox to be identified as the author of this work
has been asserted by her in accordance with the Copyright, Designs and
Patents Act 1988.

British Library Cataloguing in Publication Data
A catalogue record for this book is available from the British Library.

ISBN 1-84312-081-X

Typeset by FiSH Books
Printed and bound in Great Britain

Contents

Acknowledgements

I am indebted to all those assistants who have written to me or contributed to my thinking about their role and training needs. Much inspiration has come from their dedication and care of some of our most needy children and young people.

I would also like to thank Eleanor Olson for typing the manuscript and James Quinnell for the cartoons. And a big thank you to my own support system – Paul, Daniel, Ben, Hannah and Elizabeth.

Glenys Fox
June 2003

Purpose

The purpose of this handbook is to enable learning support assistants to work more effectively in supporting:

- the pupil with special needs;

- the class teacher and the special needs coordinator;

- the school;

- the curriculum.

Audience

This handbook is intended as a resource for:
- non-teaching staff who support pupils with special needs (usually known as learning support assistants, special needs assistants, teaching assistants, special school assistants or welfare assistants);
- non-teaching staff who come into contact with pupils who have special needs (e.g. specialist teaching assistants, classroom assistants);
- special needs coordinators and teachers who work with assistants.

Overview

There are sections on:

- the current context and statutory framework;

- roles and responsibilities;

- giving support;

- different kinds of special need;

- working with colleagues to support learning.

Introduction

During the 1990s we saw a move towards recognising the potential of learning support assistants (LSAs) in our schools. These assistants were formerly referred to as special needs assistants, special school assistants or non-teaching assistants. This 'new' name (ref: Green Paper – *Excellence for all Children*, [Department for Education and Employment] 1997) reflects the positive role these assistants play in our schools today.

Head teachers have highlighted the training and support needs of these people who are perceived by schools as having tremendous enthusiasm and dedication to children. The importance of giving support and guidance to assistants is clear. They are frequently working very closely with some very needy children whose quality of school experience can depend quite significantly on the knowledge and skills of the assistant. In addition, a good deal of skilled expertise goes into assessment and describing the needs and type of provision for children who need learning support – it follows that the delivery of any programmes described in individual education plans (IEPs) should be carried out by teachers working in partnership with assistants who have had appropriate and relevant training.

The responsibility for supporting assistants on a day-to-day basis lies primarily with class teachers working together with special needs co-ordinators (SENCOs). Head teachers have a role to play by managing school staffing arrangements to free up time both for planning and for training. The management handbook from the Audit Commission/HMI (Her Majesty's Inspectors) entitled *Getting the Act Together* (1992) recognises supporting adults as 'an expensive resource, the use of which should be prepared in advance if the cost is to be justified'. Teachers who work with LSAs have a direct influence on the deployment of this resource and should acknowledge this responsibility.

Since the publication of *A Handbook for Special Needs Assistants – working in partnership with teachers* in 1993, I have received hundreds of letters from assistants asking for details of training courses. This need for training is being increasingly recognised, resulting in the establishment of a number of training opportunities for LSAs. Many of these training courses have been locally run by Education Authority staff and by SENCOs. Others have followed more formal structures including NVQ frameworks linked to accreditation centres. The development of these courses has been patchy and the quality of content and delivery has been variable. *Excellence for all Children* (DfEE 1997) stated that:

> LSAs' careers might be enhanced by a national structure including some or all of the following:
> - national guidelines or a framework of good practice for LEAs and schools to follow;
> - an expectation that LEAs would make available accredited training for all LSAs and oversee quality assurance;
> - nationally devised modules for all LSA training courses within an NVQ framework – perhaps including a mandatory induction/foundation course, with additional modules to reflect the needs of pupils.

A qualifications framework is now emerging and assistants have a good choice of courses (see page 78). The quality control system employed will give LSAs confidence in their training programme, regardless of where they live and who is delivering the course, and provide them with a sound basis from which to work.

This current handbook has developed from *A Handbook for Special Needs Assistants – working in partnership with teachers* (1993) to recognise the changing climate of giving support to children. It is intended as a practical guide containing useful information which LSAs and teachers working with LSAs need to know and it can be used to complement training courses. It includes information about the Code of Practice published by the DfEE in 1994 and revised in 2001 as guidance to schools for use in making arrangements for meeting children's needs. Since this book was first written, much has changed in the way learning support assistants are seen as part of the education workforce. The Special Educational Needs and Disability legislation (SENDA) and the revised Code of Practice have promoted a greater degree of inclusion for children with a wide range of additional needs. This has meant an increased workload for class teachers and SENCOs and has highlighted the valuable part that LSAs have to play in the 'front line' of meeting children's day-to-day learning needs. This book describes how the resource of learning assistance can be used to best effect.

So, if you are a learning support assistant or intend to become one, or if you are a SENCO or a teacher working with an assistant, then this handbook will help you in fulfilling your particular support role.

CHAPTER 1

Special educational needs

In your work as a learning support assistant (LSA) it will be helpful for you to understand some of the background and the framework which underpins the way children identified as having special needs are supported in our schools.

The 1981 Education Act states that: 'A child has special educational needs if he or she has a learning difficulty which may be a result of a physical or sensory disability, an emotional or behavioural problem or developmental delay' (1981 Education Act, Section 1).

What is meant by 'special educational needs'?

This significant Act helped to change ideas about children with difficulties. Before the 1981 Act, children had been categorised and labelled according to their 'handicap'. People had referred to children by such labels as 'physically handicapped', 'mentally handicapped', 'educationally sub-normal' or 'maladjusted'.

The 1981 Act:

- changed the focus away from labelling the child;
- placed the focus on the extent to which a learning difficulty stops a child from learning with other children of the same age;
- placed the focus on the child's special educational needs in terms of the special educational provision required to help them learn;
- stressed that 'special educational needs' is a relative term which arises from the interaction between a child and his or her environment.

The idea of a child's needs being related to the school's ability to meet the needs was a new perspective which helped teachers to see difficulties in learning as not always starting from within the child. Sometimes, the child does not learn because the school does not provide the learning tasks or levels of support which are necessary for learning to take place; and sometimes needs are in fact created because the school is not able to be flexible. Thus the *interaction* between the child and his or her learning environment is now considered crucial in any discussion about special educational needs.

Children who have special educational needs are currently described in terms of learning difficulties, emotional and behavioural difficulties, physical disabilities, sensory impairment, language difficulties or communication impairment. Sometimes children may have learning support needs arising from a combination of these factors.

Why do we need learning support assistants?

The 1981 Act states that:

> Where possible, all children with special educational needs should be educated in ordinary schools

and

> For integration to be effective, pupils with special needs must be engaged in all or most of the activities of the school. Some pupils with special educational needs require extra help if they are to benefit from the experiences available to all pupils.

Learning support assistants (LSAs) often provide this 'extra help' which makes it possible for children to attend ordinary schools. Since the 1981 Act, many children who might previously have been educated in special schools have been educated in ordinary (i.e. mainstream) schools. The majority of these children require some different educational arrangements for some of the time in order to make the best use of the opportunities offered to them in mainstream schools.

What is meant by 'integration' and 'inclusion'?

The 1981 Education Act referred to the 'integration' of children with special needs into mainstream schools. This meant that children previously in special schools who were thought to be able to cope with the demands of mainstream school were moved for some or all of the time into their local schools and given additional support.

Time has moved on and there is now a growing trend towards 'inclusion' rather than 'integration'. This philosophy is referred to in *Excellence for all Children* (DfEE October 1997). Inclusive education means that all children, whatever their learning support needs, learn together in age-appropriate classes in local schools. Staffing and resources are made available to all according to their needs so that every child can participate in the life of the school. Rather than individual children proving their readiness for integration, inclusion means that the school must be ready, willing and enabled to accept all children, so it is a whole-school philosophy. (Lipsky and Gartner 1996, refer to this 'readiness' idea.)

It is likely that we will see many more children who have previously been educated in special schools moving into their local mainstream schools over the next few years. This will mean some assistants will move from specialist provision into mainstream to enable these pupils to have a successful learning experience and to become true participators in their local communities.

What is the 'Code of Practice'?

The Code of Practice on the identification and assessment of special educational needs was first published by the DfEE in 1994 to give practical guidance to local education authorities (LEAs) and to the governing bodies of all maintained schools on their responsibilities towards all children with special educational needs (SEN). As part of the government's 'Programme of Action' (*Meeting Special Educational Needs: A Programme of Action* (DfEE 1998)) the Code was revised and came into force in January 2002, and extended its guidance to cover all early years settings. It sets out a series of recommendations for good practice which are flexible enough to respond to local needs and contexts, and advises the adoption of:

a strategy that recognises the various levels and complexities of need, the different responsibilities to assess and meet those needs, and the associated range and variations in provision, which will best reflect and promote common recognition of the continuum of special educational needs. (DfEE 2001: 3)

The revised Code of Practice identified five guiding principles which should underpin good practice, and these are important to LSAs as well as to teachers and senior managers:

- A child with special educational needs should have his or her needs met.
- The special educational needs of children will normally be met in mainstream schools or settings.
- The views of the child should be sought and taken into account.
- Parents/carers have a vital role to play in supporting their child's education.
- Children with special educational needs should be offered full access to a broad, balanced and relevant education, including the Foundation Stage Curriculum and the National Curriculum.

Four main groups of SEN are used in the revised Code of Practice, encompassing the full range of learning needs from 'severe' to comparatively 'mild':

- Communication and interaction: most children with SEN have some degree of difficulty in at least one of the areas of speech, language and communication. These include children with speech and language difficulties, specific learning difficulties (including dyslexia and dyspraxia) and hearing impairments. Children who demonstrate features within the autistic spectrum (ASD) and those with moderate, severe or profound learning difficulties will almost certainly be included in this grouping.
- Cognition and learning: included in this group are children who have moderate, severe or profound learning difficulties, or specific learning difficulties such as dyslexia or dyspraxia, and require specific programmes to aid progress in learning.
- Behavioural, emotional and social development: this group includes children who seem depressed or isolated, those whose behaviour is disruptive and challenging and those who self-harm. Children who appear hyperactive and lack the ability to concentrate may also form part of this group, as will those with immature social skills.
- Sensory and/or physical: this group encompasses children with a wide range of sensory, multisensory and physical difficulties. The range extends from profound and permanent deafness or visual impairment, to lesser levels of loss and through a continuum of mobility and coordination difficulties.

It is important to recognise that a child's needs often overlap these groups and the important issue is meeting individual needs, regardless of which group or category they fall into.

The Code of Practice sets out a 'graduated response' to meeting children's needs and these steps are described as 'School (or Early Years) Action' and 'School (or Early Years) Action Plus'. If a child is not making appropriate progress after these two stages, the parents/carers or school can request the LEA to make a 'statutory assessment' which may lead to the issuing of a statement.

School (or Early Years) Action

This action may be triggered when a child is not making progress in spite of the class teacher giving him a little more attention and differentiated work (this means work that is closely matched to his ability and allows him to succeed). An important part of the process is to share concerns with the child's parents/carers to find out if they have extra information about the child and to involve them where possible in actively supporting his educational development. The SENCO will usually become involved and suggest to the teacher ways in which the child can be helped – possibly including some additional support from an LSA. An Individual Education Plan (IEP) will be drawn up to focus on specific targets for the child.

School (or Early Years) Action Plus

If the child is not making progress in spite of the strategies used as part of School Action, the SENCO will contact one or more specialists from outside agencies. These may be professionals from the LEA support services, area Health Authority, Social Services or independent consultants: educational psychologists, speech therapists, literacy consultants, learning support advisors and behaviour management experts. Where more than one specialist is consulted they should work together as a team, with the school and the child's parents, to devise and implement an effective programme. These outside consultants will often carry out detailed assessments of the child's needs and then advise staff about an appropriate course of action, with suitable targets for IEPs and a system for monitoring progress. It is rare for them to become directly involved in teaching a child; the class teacher and/or SENCO is usually responsible for the delivery of interventions, often with input from an assistant.

What is an Individual Education Plan? (IEP)

This is a teaching and learning plan for the child drawn up by the SEN coordinator working with the child's teacher, the LSA, and possibly with ideas from parents, advisory teachers or educational psychologists.

According to the Code of Practice the plan should be formulated as follows:

- nature of the child's learning difficulties;
- action – the special educational provision;
  - staff involved, including frequency of support;
  - specific programmes/activities/materials/equipment;
- help from parents at home;
- targets to be achieved in a given time;
- any pastoral care or medical requirements;
- monitoring and assessment arrangements;
- review arrangements and date.

The recommendation is that the plan should be frequently reviewed to see if it is working well. If not then the targets and special arrangements should be changed.

In spite of a range of interventions at School Action and School Action Plus, there may come a point when everyone concerned with the child decides that he is not making progress and a statutory assessment of need may be requested. This may or may not lead to a 'Statement of Special Educational Needs', a legal document which specifies the 'additional' or 'special' resources to be provided for the child. Many assistants currently work for some or all of their time with pupils who have statements.

It is part of an LEA's duty to consider every application for statutory assessment, but they may turn down a request if it is not backed up by evidence from the school that appropriate steps have already been taken to help the child at School Action and School Action Plus. The school should provide details of IEPs used with the child, records of regular reviews, details of attainment in learning (especially literacy and numeracy), views of the parents/carers and of the child, reports from external agencies and medical history where appropriate. The SEN

What is a 'Statement'?

Thresholds provide guidance on putting together this information and enable comparisons to be made between provision for children with similar needs in different schools and different authorities.

If the LEA agrees on a statutory, multi-disciplinary assessment, new reports are requested from the educational psychologist and all the other agencies involved with the child, including a school medical officer. All of this information is considered by the LEA panel who then decide whether or not to issue a statement. When a statement is written, it usually specifies an amount and the type of help the child should receive in school that requires significant additional resources, or it recommends a place in a specialist setting. The parents have a right to appeal against any decision made by the LEA which they do not agree with, at any stage of the process. If any disagreement cannot be resolved locally, the case may be referred to the Special Educational Needs Tribunal for a decision to be made.

The Code of Practice guides schools in providing support from their own resources for the vast majority of children with special educational needs and advocates statutory assessment only for pupils who have severe and complex needs.

CHAPTER 2

The role of the
learning support assistant

In your work as an assistant you will be working as part of the learning support team in the school which is led by the special needs coordinator (SENCO). If you work in a large school then there may be several teachers employed to give learning support but in small schools there is usually only one teacher with such a role and that is the SENCO. When we talk of learning support this usually refers to additional help over and above what most children need. In its widest sense all teachers give learning support to all children and certainly all class teachers have the responsibility for the learning programmes of all children in their classes whatever their learning needs.

What are my responsibilities?

It is important for you to remember that LSAs are not teachers and should never be overburdened in terms of responsibilities. The class teacher has the responsibility for the education of all children in his or her class and the head teacher has the responsibility for all the children in the school.

If you are working with children who need different arrangements, the class teacher has the responsibility to ensure that appropriate programmes are planned, followed and monitored. These will usually be detailed on the child's IEP or in group work arrangements. As an assistant, you are expected to work under the guidance of the class teacher to meet the needs of the child. There may be occasions when you are expected to work on your own with one or more children. In this situation you need to work as a responsible adult in ensuring the well-being of each child.

In particular lessons there will be particular routines to follow, e.g. when supporting a pupil in food technology you may need to have an appropriate health and safety certificate. There will be a member of staff in your school who is responsible for health and safety and who can give you advice about this. There are guidelines for staff who accompany children off site and for staff who may be involved in administering drugs to children. Your SENCO should be able to direct you to any information needed.

Every employee of the local authority is covered by a general employment insurance policy held by that authority. By law, you are deemed 'a

What if something goes wrong?

responsible adult' and the duties performed by you are delegated to you by the head teacher. If something does go wrong, you should discuss the situation with the teacher who is responsible for your work and with the head teacher. In the case of any accident, it must be recorded in the schools' incident/accident book. In the case of injury to a child, your first priority is to see that the child is given first aid and that the class teacher is informed.

If, during the course of your work with a child, some disclosure of physical or sexual abuse is made, then you have a duty, under Child Protection law, to inform the head teacher who will take any action necessary. The 1989 Children Act states that the child's welfare is paramount and safeguarding it and promoting it is a priority.

Schools have clear routines to be followed in the case of injury or abuse and it is your responsibility to ensure that you know what these procedures are. If you are not sure, the class teacher you normally work with can direct you to the information.

You may consider that membership of a union will be useful in providing you with back-up support, should things go badly wrong.

What might I be asked to do?

The role of the learning support assistant will vary from school to school, depending on the organisation and on the individual child, or groups of children, concerned. It is important that you know what your duties are from the start in relation to different pupils. You need to know whether you are working mainly with one child or are expected to work with small groups, or sometimes with the whole class.

Some of the more usual tasks assistants are asked to do are as follows:

- explaining points and repeating instructions given by the teacher;
- producing worksheets and resources for the pupil, in consultation with the teacher;
- reading stories to children on an individual or small group basis or hearing them read;
- playing a game with a child or small group;
- making notes for the pupil as the teacher is speaking which can be used in the work which follows;
- checking the work pupils produce and helping them to correct their own mistakes;
- acting as a scribe;
- helping younger children change for PE (or older pupils who have physical disabilities);
- explaining words the child does not understand, encouraging use of dictionaries;
- guiding computer-assisted learning programmes;
- preparing audio-tapes and encouraging the use of a Dictaphone for recording information – you may need to transcribe what the pupil dictates;
- reading textbook sections or questions to the pupil;
- supervising practical work;
- helping the pupil catch up on missed work;
- observing a child's way of managing a task – only intervening if the child cannot do it independently;

- keeping the pupil and others 'on task';
- reporting back to the teacher, especially problems or successes;
- contributing to planning and review meetings about the pupil;
- helping children learn spellings;
- sharing books with children.

It is sometimes the case that LSAs are 'thrown in at the deep end' with no clear idea of what is expected of them.

If you are not clear about what you are expected to do then you do need to ask. Confusion can be prevented by:

- a clear job description (see Appendix A);

'It's O.K. Off you go – you'll be all right'

- communication between the class teacher and the assistant so that the assistant is clear about:
  - the ground rules for working with the teacher;
  - the individual plan for the pupil (IEP).

What are the ground rules?

These are guidelines for you to use in working with a particular teacher. They should be discussed with teachers before you start work as an assistant or, for experienced assistants, when working with a new teaching colleague.

Teachers will have their own ideas and you need to ask about these before you start, so that you can reduce confusion and provide a consistent approach. Also, you need to know what authority you have when working in the classroom. The more you understand the workings of the class and the way the teacher operates, the easier it will be for you to work within the class and to support the children who need help.

Here are some suggestions of questions to ask in order to determine 'ground rules':

1. **How shall I be introduced to the class?**

   It is important that you are, in fact, introduced to the class at the beginning of the school year rather than being treated as a piece of furniture. It is also important that you are introduced in the right way so that pupils' perception of your role is clear. Discuss this with the class teacher.

   An introduction such as: 'This is Mrs Smith and she is Andrew's special helper' is probably not helpful, both in terms of Andrew being pointed out as 'special' and of raising the idea of Mrs Smith as some kind of 'minder'. A more useful introduction might be: 'This is Mrs Smith who will be working with me to help you all to do your best. Sometimes, she will work with one or two of you and sometimes with small groups.'

2. **How do I work with other pupils?**

   Even though you may be only responsible for one pupil, the others will note your presence and will be curious. You should be prepared to tell them something about yourself and, as far as possible, treat all pupils in the class in, generally, the same way, giving help to them as well as to your pupil, if they ask for it. You should encourage them to accept your pupil as a full member of the class.

3. **Can I give pupils 'permission'?**

   e.g. When a child asks to go to the toilet, can I give permission? It is likely that children will ask your permission on frequent occasions about how to act in certain situations. Discuss any such scenarios with the class teacher so that you know what to do.

4. **Can I 'mark' books?**

   e.g. When a child comes to show me some written work, when is it appropriate for me to put a mark on their work? It is likely that this will be acceptable for you to do when working individually or in small groups with children but, generally, the class teacher will need to do this.

5. **Where shall I sit in the classroom?**

   e.g. When is it appropriate for me to sit right by the pupil and when should I stay at a distance? This will depend on the particular activity and you will learn, with practice, when it is necessary to give individual support and when to withdraw and allow the pupil some independence.

6. **What shall I do if I see some misbehaviour?**

   e.g. When two children are getting at each other, shall I intervene and, if so, what sort of approach should I use? There are bound to be occasions when you see things going on of which the teacher is unaware. You need to negotiate with the class teacher how you should react to such situations, and know when it is appropriate to refer the situation to the class teacher rather than deal with it yourself.

7. **Can I contribute or ask questions during the lesson?**

   There may be times when you feel you can add particular bits of information which will add to a class discussion. You may also feel the need to ask for clarification – possibly for yourself or, more often, if you can see that the pupil is not clear. However, do avoid becoming 'the overgrown pupil' in the classroom (described by M. Balshaw in her book *Help in the Classroom*).

Avoid becoming the 'overgrown pupil'

8. **What is the best use of my time?**

   e.g. Should I sit in on school assemblies when I am not really needed? You need to negotiate a timetable which is able to use your support to best effect and to agree with the teacher when your presence is needed and when it might be of more use for you to be preparing materials for the pupil or pupils you support, e.g. in assembly time.

9. **Will I be expected to talk to parents?**

   You may well be seen as an extra source of information by parents who approach you at the school gate, in the playground, or even at the supermarket. They may want to know about their own child's progress, complain about other children's behaviour, or even criticise the class teacher. It is important to be professional at times like this and not jeopardise your relationships with colleagues. Practise a way of being polite but firm, e.g. 'I will pass that on to Mrs Smith and ask her to have a word with you'. Confidentiality is an important issue and you should discuss with the teacher what is for 'broadcasting' and what is not.

10. **Will there be time for planning?**

    There is never enough time in any school for planning, but it is important to know what is going to happen in lessons and how you can be most effective. Work out with teachers how to find time for planning so that you can discuss the pupils you will be working with and how you will support them. Ask for copies of lesson/topic plans if possible.

11. **How can I be effective in lessons?**

    You will be dependent on the skills of the teacher to some extent, and on how well he or she deploys you. You need to be clear about what the pupils you are working with are expected to learn by the end of the lesson. It will be an important part of your job to find out how best to work with each pupil, according to their needs, and how much to expect of them – not too much, and not too little. Remember that you should be helping them to learn 'on their own' – weaning them off support if at all possible – so beware of making them too dependent on you.

CHAPTER 3

Giving support

When learning support assistants are asked to define their supporting role, their responses fall into four main categories:

- supporting the pupil;
- supporting the teacher;
- supporting the curriculum;
- supporting the school.

LSAs identify the following aspects of their supportive role with pupils:

- promoting independence;
- inspiring confidence and trust;
- valuing the child;
- fostering peer group acceptance;
- encouraging and giving rewards;
- developing listening skills;
- enabling the child;
- knowing the background;
- finding out about the learning support needs;
- keeping confidences;
- being 'in tune' with the child's physical needs.

How can I support the pupil?

Promoting independence

This is a key concept in considering your role. You are there to give a high level of support initially, but as time goes on, you must be seeking to encourage the pupil to attempt new tasks without your support. It is common for LSAs to feel that they must always be 'one step ahead' but, in fact, the idea of being 'one step behind' is much more helpful in promoting the independence of the pupil. If you are always foreseeing pitfalls and removing them from the path of the pupil, then he or she will never learn strategies for coping in the real world.

However, there will be times when you will have to act in order to pre-empt serious situations – common sense is a necessary quality!

Some learning support assistants feel that if they are employed to work with one particular pupil, then it is appropriate to 'stick like glue' to that pupil. Though there are times when the child will need individual support, it will often be appropriate to help the pupil within a small group or even to spend time standing back and observing the behaviour of the pupil in classroom situations. You may be surprised at how much he or she is capable of. You will be doing the child no favours if you encourage dependence on you. In fact, you should be aiming to be so effective in promoting the independence of the pupil that you work yourself out of a job!

Inspiring confidence and trust

Often, it is the case that pupils with special educational needs are lacking in confidence. Children become aware of failure very quickly and they lose confidence when they see their classmates making progress while they struggle. Pupils who have had difficult social histories may feel that they have been 'let down' by the important adults in their lives and feel it is hard to trust someone to be consistent, fair and encouraging. A pupil with a low opinion of himself or herself, for whatever reason, is going to begin to expect to fail. It is, therefore, vital that you take every opportunity to point out what the pupil is good at and to lead them to expect that they can succeed. Think out ways of providing frequent opportunities for real success. It may take time but if you have a consistent, positive and fair attitude towards the child, he or she will learn to develop confidence and to trust you.

Valuing the child

No child can learn effectively when they are not feeling valued. It is a key role of a learning support assistant to value the child. Any child who is thought of as 'different' from other pupils may encounter negative

Wow!

attitudes particularly if the disability is obvious. Surviving childhood teasing is often dependent on self-esteem, so it is very important that the child feels secure and highly regarded by the important people in his or her life and you are one of them.

Fostering peer group acceptance

It is part of your role to encourage the other pupils to value the child. This entails drawing attention to those skills the child is good at, or to some particular achievement of the child. It may also involve valuing the contributions of the child, e.g. making the child group leader in appropriate activities. Some children need help to improve social skills, i.e. the way they relate to others. If the child you work with has poor social skills then you can help him or her by practising appropriate responses – first in play-acting then in real situations. For younger children it might be helpful to act out a well-known fairy tale, e.g. Billy Goats Gruff, with each child being able to take on different roles. This can help children explore feelings and relationships – the troll seen as a 'bully' and the little billy goat Gruff seen as the 'victim'. This sort of activity can lead on to discussions about feelings and rights and wrongs. For older pupils, discussing real situations and then role-playing to consider the best outcomes can be extremely helpful.

Encouraging and giving rewards

Giving the pupil encouragement and praise is a very important part of your role and will contribute in a large part to the development of self-esteem and confidence. Liberal amounts of praise must be given. Meaningful praise means telling the pupil why you are pleased with him or her, e.g. it is better to say 'Gemma, I like the way you have used colour in this picture' rather than 'That's a good picture', or 'Tom, you listened to the story well today' rather than just 'Good boy'.

All children respond to rewards if the rewards are motivating and achievable. It will help you in your work with the pupil if you can work out, early on in your relationship, something tangible. Here are some ideas you might suggest to the child as incentives, but remember to ask the child first what they would like as a reward once they have achieved what you have negotiated.

Ideas for rewards

Primary age pupils

- extra 'choosing time', when he or she can choose an activity;
- extra time on the computer;
- a favourite game;
- a bubble-blowing session;
- making biscuits, cakes or sweets;
- stickers to wear and keep;
- decorating plain biscuits with icing and 'sprinkles';

- doing an 'important' job for the class teacher or head teacher;
- music while you work;
- letter or certificate sent home to parents.

Secondary age pupils

- extra time on the computer;
- letter or certificate sent home to parents;
- position of responsibility;
- a special interest project;
- free ticket to school disco.

It is important to ensure that the reward is achievable over a short period of time to start with, so that success is encouraged. For younger children particularly, the reward needs to be earned within one day so that it is immediate. Other children may be able to work towards a reward at the end of two or three days, or at the end of a week. Again, you will need to negotiate this with the class teacher so that there is consistency in your approach.

Developing listening skills

When you start work with a pupil, it is tempting to do a lot of the talking and to expect that the pupil has taken in what you have said. Remember that effective communication is a two-way process and that some children need time to get their thoughts together and to express themselves. Some are only able to understand short bits of information at a time. You may need to check that the pupil has understood by asking him or her to repeat back to you the information you have given or that the teacher has given to the class. This simple technique is called 'perception checking' and is an extremely valuable skill to practise and use regularly.

Pupils with emotional difficulties can be helped enormously by someone providing a 'listening ear'. This means that when the pupil is talking, you give him or her your full attention and are able to make encouraging gestures such as nodding and smiling. Non-verbal 'messages' from you to the child are, in fact, more important than the words you use.

You can learn to encourage pupils to talk by choosing the right phrases. This is called Active Listening. Brenda Mallon, in her book *An Introduction to Counselling for Special Educational Needs*, gives the following examples:

Listening skills		
Types	*Purpose*	*Examples*
Warmth, Support	To help the pupil	'I'd like to help you; are you able to tell me about what is the matter?'
Clarification	To get the complete 'story' from the pupil	'Can you tell me more about it?' 'Do you mean...............?'
Restatement	To check our meaning is the same as the pupil's	'From what you are saying, I understand that..................'
Encouragement	To encourage the pupil	'I realise this is difficult for you but you are doing really well'
Reflective	To act as a mirror so the pupil can see what is being communicated	'You feel that..............' 'It was very hard for you to accept.................'
	To help pupils evaluate their feelings	'You felt angry and upset when....................'
	To show you understand the feelings behind the words	'I can see you are feeling upset....................'
Summarising	To bring together the points raised	'These are the main things you have told me............' 'As I see it, your main worry seems to be.................'

If you are able to use some of these skills then you will be well on the way to being a good listener and, more than that, you will help the pupil to work through whatever is causing worry or concern.

Enabling the child

The pupil who needs learning support often feels unable to attempt tasks which other pupils have no problem with. Your role is not to do the task for the pupil, but to enable the pupil to do that task for himself or herself by providing the necessary 'tools for the job'. This may mean:

- explaining the task clearly when the pupil has not understood (if the problem persists, see the teacher);
- making sure the pupil knows what equipment is necessary, where it is kept and how to use it;
- helping the pupil to organise his/her thoughts and consider how to set out the work;
- encouraging the pupil to arrive at the lesson on time and with the correct equipment;
- giving the pupil strategies to use to help him/her remember information, e.g. writing lists, keeping a diary;
- working with small groups to encourage sharing and cooperation.

Your role is *not* to do the task for the pupil!

You may need to adapt the worksheet provided by the teacher so that the pupil can understand and do the task. Making a task simpler in this way is called differentiation and it is done so that the child is more likely to understand and learn.

Your role is not to do the task for the pupil

Knowing the background

You will understand the pupil's difficulties better if you know something about the pupil's home life and the way he or she spends time out of school.

It will help you in establishing a relationship if you find out early on who the other family members are, whether the pupil has any pets and what hobbies or special interests he or she has. You may find it valuable, particularly with younger children, to keep a scrapbook entitled 'All About Me', into which you can put photographs and snippets of written information about what happens in the life of the child. The child will feel valued when you show interest in the things which are meaningful to him or her. For the older child this can also be a useful activity. Writing an autobiography 'My Life Story', can be particularly helpful to pupils who have emotional difficulties and low self-esteem.

Finding out about the learning support needs

It is the responsibility of the class teacher or the special needs coordinator in the school to ensure that you know what you need to know about the child's particular needs, in order to do the job. If you feel you don't know, do ask. There is likely to be a list of children with special educational

Show an interest in the child's interests ...

needs in the school together with individual education plans. There is a network of services external to the school, e.g. speech and language therapists, physiotherapists, teacher advisers, educational psychologists and child psychiatrists who can be approached, together with your class teacher, should you want to find out more information. There are also many charitable organisations which offer information about a wide range of disabilities, e.g. SCOPE (formerly the Spastics Society) and the Royal National Institute for the Blind. (Appendix B provides more information about the roles of supporting professionals.)

The information contained in the child's school records will give you some background knowledge. You will need to check with the head teacher whether you can have access to this information.

Keeping confidences

This follows on well from the last point. When you work closely with a child, there are bound to be times when you hear or see information, e.g. about the child's home life, which must be kept confidential. This does not apply, however, to disclosure of child abuse, which is information you have a duty to share with the head teacher. In the course of your job, you may find people confiding in you. While you can discuss information with other professionals concerned, please remember that the information you come across in the course of your job is not for discussion or comment with outsiders.

Being 'in tune' with the child's physical needs

This refers to the physical well-being of the child. There are occasions when a child comes to school feeling tired, hungry or just not well. This is particularly the case with pupils who have physical disabilities and who may have had disturbed sleep. Children from non-nurturing homes are also at risk. When working with such children, the session is not always likely to be an academic success. Don't feel you have failed if nothing is achieved on paper sometimes – quite often, showing a genuine interest in the child and lending a sympathetic ear goes a long way towards compensating for what may be lacking in the child's background. Be aware of any moodiness or lethargy and make allowances for it. Imagine how you feel yourself when you are tired or run-down, and treat the child with gentleness and sensitivity. When working with secondary age pupils you may need to be alert to signs of drug taking and be prepared to report back if you are concerned.

How can I support the teacher?

LSAs identified the following aspects of their supportive role with respect to the class teacher:

- working in partnership;
- providing feedback about the how the pupil manages the work given;
- helping in setting targets, monitoring and evaluating IEPs;
- recording information;
- maintaining a sense of humour.

Working in partnership

Working in any partnership implies *communication*. In order to work well with a class teacher you must feel able to ask questions, clarify expectations and get feedback on your work with the pupil. It is a two-way process and obviously much depends on the personality and organisational skills of the teacher, on whom you are dependent for direction and guidance.

However, if you are to work effectively it is vital that you meet regularly for information exchange, joint planning and evaluation. In a primary school it need only be for a short time each day or each week but it is in the best interests of the pupils that you do this. In a secondary school this is more difficult as you may be supporting the pupil in up to ten curriculum areas. You may find it more practical to have one longer planning session per month. Planning does take some time commitment by the class teacher but you will be better able to support him or her if you are both clear about what you are both doing.

To quote from the Audit Commission/HMI handbook: 'Where extra help is provided, planning and communication are the keys to improving its impact.' This document also stresses the need for the supporting adult to 'be aware of the class teacher's objectives for a piece of work so that he or she can then focus on what the child is to master, and consider alternative means of reaching the same goal.'

Working in partnership can be a problem, particularly for LSAs who work in secondary schools who will have to work with a number of different teachers. Some staff may have subject specialisms and it may be sometimes necessary for you to ensure that a member of staff understands the way in which you can assist a pupil in a given situation and the limitations of that pupil.

A small minority of teachers feel threatened by the presence of another adult in the classroom. If you feel uncomfortable about any situation it may help to discuss your concerns with the special needs coordinator and the teacher concerned. But do remember that your main role is not to give 'marks out of ten' for the quality of any lesson or any teaching style, but to act in the best interests of the pupils whom you are employed to support and enable them to make the best of any teaching situation.

Providing feedback about the pupil

In working closely with a particular pupil or group of pupils, it is likely that you will be more sensitive to their needs and reactions in any given situation than is the class teacher, who takes a wider view.

You will be able, therefore, to provide information to the teacher about how well the pupil is coping with the demands made on him or her. This may involve written feed back or record keeping. If a task given to the pupil is too difficult, please don't feel you must persevere with it to the bitter end but feed back to the teacher that this is the case and either get the teacher to modify the task or agree that you yourself can do this. Learning support assistants are often wonderfully creative given the opportunity, so feel confident in making suggestions and modifications as you feel necessary. The majority of teachers will be only too pleased to hear your ideas and take them on board if possible.

In addition to feedback about how the pupil is coping with school work you will also be able to provide information about the general well-being of the pupil and about situations out of school or in the playground which may be affecting the pupil's performance in class.

Helping in setting targets, monitoring and evaluating programmes

In an ideal situation, when you are meeting regularly with the class teacher or special needs coordinator, you will be able to make a contribution to the planning of individual education plans (see Chapter 1). It is the responsibility of the class teacher and possibly the special needs coordinator to do this for each pupil with special needs, as they might be deciding exactly what is the next step for the pupil. You will be able to contribute ideas about how this might be done, bearing in mind the temperament of the pupil.

It is also extremely valuable to *evaluate* what you are doing with the pupil. This means 'taking a step back' periodically, say every half term, or even more frequently, and asking yourself just how effective your work with the pupil has been and whether the targets or goals set have been achieved. If not, or only partially, it would be worth discussing alternative approaches with the class teacher in order to see if this makes a difference.

But do remember that many children who need learning support often learn only slowly and so realistic expectations are clearly needed.

Recording information

As part of your work in supporting the teacher, it is essential that you record what you do in the course of your work with the pupils. The class teacher or special needs coordinator will be able to advise you about the sort of records you should keep and the format this should take. The information you will be asked to record will depend on the particular needs of the pupil. For instance, you may be asked to record details about the language the child uses or about how many times he or she shows aggressive behaviour. Whatever the record is, it should contain useful information to help in planning future work rather than just a diary of events. So it might, therefore, be useful to record the date, the activity and the materials used, bearing in mind why you are doing the task. It would then be useful to record an evaluative comment about how well the pupil succeeded in the task. In any record, it is very important to record successes as well as difficulties. Feeding back success to the teacher will improve the motivation of the child.

Consider:

* Has the pupil learned?
  If not, why not? (task too hard, wrong time of day, too many distractions, unmotivating materials, etc.);
* How might this be done better next time? (Discuss with teacher.)

Maintaining a sense of humour

When a teacher has a pupil or pupils with special needs in his or her class it can sometimes become hard work as progress is often slow and the level of attention demanded by these pupils is often high. For the health and sanity of the teacher, the pupil and yourself it is a good thing to smile and joke about situations which invite it. Do not allow situations to become too 'heavy' – having a sense of optimism and good humour can help the teacher and the pupils enormously. Do avoid using sarcasm as this can be damaging to the self-esteem of the pupil.

Mutual support of teacher and learning support assistant can be of tremendous benefit.

Suggestion to enhance mutual support

Take some time to sit down with the teacher(s) you work with and do the following exercise:

I am a learning support assistant. How can I best support the teacher?
I am a teacher. How can I best support the learning support assistant?

LSAs identify the following aspects of their supportive role in respect of the curriculum:

- developing a knowledge of the curriculum which the pupils are expected to follow;
- becoming familiar with the National Strategies and their implications for the pupils;
- developing the skills to adapt subject-based activities to meet the needs of the pupils.

How can I support the curriculum?

Developing a knowledge of the curriculum

All pupils follow the National Curriculum. This describes the programmes of study in each subject which every child and young person in England should be taught. It is divided into four Key Stages:

Nursery and Year R (reception)	Foundation Stage
Key Stage 1 for pupils in Years R (reception), 1, 2	} Primary Stage
Key Stage 2 for pupils in Years 3, 4, 5, 6	
Key Stage 3 for pupils in Years 7, 8, 9	} Secondary Stage
Key Stage 4 for pupils in Years 10, 11	

The curriculum has five core subjects: English, mathematics, science, religious education and information and communications technology (ICT); and eight foundation subjects: history, geography, modern foreign languages, design technology, art and design, physical education, music, and personal, social and health education (PSHE). All pupils with special educational needs follow the curriculum, although those children who have severe and complex needs are often said to be 'working towards' some of the targets set in the curriculum.

If you are an assistant working in a primary or special school it will be important for you to learn about the range of subjects taught so you will be better able to support the pupils with correct facts and explanations. In some secondary schools, assistants are becoming attached to specific curriculum areas and are becoming very knowledgeable about certain subjects, as they learn with the pupils. You may feel under-confident at first, but do remember to ask if you are not clear. If you do not understand what is being taught, then it is likely that the pupil does not understand either. Do beware, however, of becoming an 'overgrown pupil', and know when it is appropriate to contribute, or not.

Becoming familiar with the National Strategies

The Department for Education and Skills has introduced a number of strategies to support the progress of pupils in English schools. These are the Literacy and Numeracy Strategies at Key Stages 1 and 2 (the Primary Strategy) and the Key Stage 3 Strategy for secondary-aged pupils at Key Stage 3. These strategies provide materials and activities aimed at improving pupils' literacy, numeracy and ICT skills. You may be asked to use some of these activities designed specifically for pupils who are low achievers and who may have some special educational needs. The teachers you work with will be able to guide you in the use of these units and modules of work.

Developing the skills to adapt subject-based activities

Children do not all learn at the same rate; they have different abilities and aptitudes. In getting to know the pupils you work with, you will become aware of their individual strengths and weaknesses. You will develop a secure knowledge of what they can manage and of how information should be presented so that the pupil becomes a successful learner. You will therefore find it necessary to adapt activities and worksheets for certain pupils; for example, enlarging maps in a geography lesson for a pupil with a visual impairment, or simplifying a written task in an English lesson by providing the first words of each sentence.

How can I support the school?

LSAs identify the following aspects of their supportive role within the school:

- working as part of the learning support 'team';
- working with parents;
- contributing to reviews;
- knowing the school procedures;
- attending relevant in-service training or staff meetings;
- using particular personal strengths.

By working as part of the learning support 'team'

Within the school this team will consist of the class teacher(s), the learning support assistants and the special needs coordinator, who has a general overview of all pupils in the school who need learning support. In secondary schools the year head and class tutor may also have a role. The head teacher has overall responsibility for you and may take an active interest, but usually the role of supervision is delegated to the special needs coordinator or class teacher.

There are other professionals whose workbase is outside the school but who come into school regularly to give advice about pupils with special needs and are therefore part of a wider support network. These include educational psychologists, physiotherapists, occupational therapists, speech and language therapists and advisory teachers. These people will

'Ahem! Friends, parents and countrymen ... '

be pleased to discuss with you any relevant issues related to your work. (See Appendix B.)

In an ideal situation, you will feel valued and supported if colleagues in the school see you as part of a team. Giving you the opportunity to be involved in planning and decision-making will encourage your own ideas and creativity and you will feel more positive about your role in the school. This depends largely on the attitudes of other members of staff, some of whom may find partnership-working too threatening and are thus unable to treat you as having a different but equal contribution to make. More usually, however, it is because staff are too busy to step back from their daily work and plan ahead with you. Too often, learning support assistants are placed in a 'reactive' role – responding to whatever comes up at the time without any planning, rather than a 'proactive' role – taking time to plan intervention in advance.

In order to make the best use of your time, a teamwork approach is vital. Very few teachers would disagree with this. If you feel you are a 'reactive' LSA then discuss with the class teacher and/or special needs coordinator any ideas you might have about improving how your time is used and how you feel the need to be part of a team.

The parents or home carers of the pupils concerned also play a part in this teamwork approach. It is important that they are made aware of the programmes and plans which are being made for their children so that they can be encouraged to support the work of the school at home in whatever way is appropriate. The most important adults in a child's life are the parents and their influence on the child is enormous. It is important that they understand the implications of any difficulty and are helped to be positive in their attitudes and expectations.

'Sorry, did no-one tell you the trip's been postponed until next week?'

Working with parents or carers

Your job may bring you into frequent contact with the child's parents or carers, particularly if the child has physical disabilities. In some cases an important part of your role may be to develop a positive relationship with the parents and to foster links between home and school, working in partnership with the class teacher. At times, it may be necessary to provide a 'listening ear' in order to support the parents and to understand what is going on in the child's home life. It is necessary to keep a safe distance emotionally when this happens and to beware of getting embroiled in complex family dynamics. It is also necessary to keep confidences which may be shared. The class teacher should be aware of relevant issues and should be able to intervene should things become too 'heavy'. Sometimes it is very hard for parents to accept that their child has a special need. You may have a part to play in helping them to come to terms with this and to be realistic. Valuing what a child is good at and pointing out progress may be part of your role in such a situation.

Contributing to reviews

Every pupil who has a statement of special educational needs must have a review of their special educational needs, at least annually. This includes a meeting when all concerned with the pupil, both inside the school and outside, can come together, discuss recent reports, inform each other about progress and make plans for meeting the pupil's needs in the future. Pupils without statements may also have internal review meetings.

'Saint or superwoman? – or both!'

If you have had close contact with the pupil, you may be asked to give a short verbal or written report at the meeting and if you have kept records they will prove useful in giving your report. Do remember that there will always be people within the school who will help you to do this and opportunities for you to discuss your contribution before the meeting.

Occasionally there will be case conferences about children with whom you are involved. Such meetings normally follow a pupil's exclusion from school or some concern voiced by the health department or social services. Again you may be asked to give your perspective about the pupil's needs. On rare occasions, you could be asked to give your views on a child's needs and progress for court hearings. Your teacher colleagues will support you in doing this. It is important that you give your views in line with the school views about the child's needs following preparation and discussion of the issues.

Knowing the school procedures

You will be able to support the school effectively if you make sure you know about school policies and procedures, e.g. accidents, discipline, bullying, out of school visits, child protection etc. Ask the head teacher what procedures you need to know of if you are unsure.

There will also be ongoing procedural changes. It is unlikely that you will attend all staff meetings (which are normally held outside the LSA contracted hours) so in order to be aware of week-by-week changes, you need to refer to a member of staff, probably the special needs coordinator, who should make you aware of changes, particularly if they affect you. Again, *communication* is the key factor.

Attending relevant in-service training or staff meetings

When opportunities arise to further your knowledge about learning support or to be involved in meetings about whole-school initiatives, then do try to attend. Ideally, this time should come from within your school hours – in reality many LSAs choose to work additional hours in order that their pupils do not miss out.

This need for training is now being recognised, and provided for in many areas.

By using particular personal strengths

The whole class and maybe the school can benefit if you are prepared to share any particular talent you might have. It could be that you are a good singer or can play an instrument well. Perhaps you have artistic or dramatic talent or maybe your culinary or D.I.Y. skills are renowned. Don't hide your light under a bushel – be willing to contribute. And don't underestimate the parenting skills you may have – the vast majority of LSAs are parents themselves so can often provide insights about what might be appropriate to solve common childhood problems.

What makes an effective learning support assistant?

The following qualities were described by a group of learning support assistants:

- patience;
- care;
- sense of fairness;
- consistency;
- sensitivity;
- ability to learn from mistakes;
- flexibility;
- versatility;
- positive attitudes;
- friendliness;
- being hard to shock;
- sense of humour;
- enthusiasm.

Most LSAs possess many of these qualities and become aware of areas which need to be worked on.

CHAPTER 4

The role of the special needs coordinator in working with the learning support assistant

Since the introduction of the Code of Practice, the role of special needs coordinator (SENCO) has become much more prescribed as a coordinator of learning support and as a manager of systems and resources. The revised Code of Practice reinforces this ideal. For many SENCOs, a significant part of their role now involves managing and advising a team of learning support assistants and helping them to work in partnership with teaching staff.

When SENCOs are asked what is good practice in working with learning support assistants, they identify the following guidelines as important.
SENCOs should ensure that assistants are:

How can SENCOs make best use of learning support assistance?

- clear about roles and responsibilities;
- valued as part of the learning support team;
- given regular opportunities for planning with teacher colleagues;
- clear about learning objectives;
- clear about the learning and emotional implications of the child's special need;
- deployed efficiently, effectively and flexibly;
- given opportunities for training and development.

Clear about roles and responsibilities

An important part of your role as SENCO is to provide a clear *job description* (see Appendix A) which describes the LSA's duties in four areas:

- supporting the pupil;
- supporting the teacher;
- supporting the curriculum;
- supporting the school.

This can be extremely useful in setting the framework within which the LSA will work. Fundamental to this is an understanding of the *purpose* of assistance which is to assist and support inclusion of children with special educational needs within the school. It will be important at the outset to make clear to assistants the degree of sensitivity which this implies – that the job is not to be a minder or a personal servant for the pupil but to encourage independence and self-reliance. Certainly it needs to be made clear that the LSA is not there to do the work for the pupil and that sometimes allowing the pupil to get things wrong might be a valuable part of a learning experience.

In doing their job, assistants will value your advice on the practical aspects of working as an extra adult in the classroom in order to avoid feeling uncomfortable or, worse still, unwanted! Certain ground rules will need to be established with the class teacher (subject teachers, if in secondary) and the SENCO can arrange for this to be negotiated at the start of a school year so that the assistant does not feel 'thrown in at the deep end'. (See Chapter 2 for Ground Rules.)

As SENCO you will also need to ensure that the assistants understand routines and procedures which operate within the school – from child protection to fire drill – and more local systems, such as reading schemes and library use.

Another consideration is that of responsibility for the learning programme (IEP). LSAs should be made aware that it is not their responsibility to devise, develop, monitor and evaluate the learning programmes for the child but that their main role will be to facilitate the implementation of the programme. It is good practice for the assistants to be involved at all these stages and to be confident enough to add their observations and ideas to any programme. The professional responsibility however, lies with the class teacher and special needs coordinator. Assistants should not be overburdened in this respect.

Valued as part of the learning support team

Any management textbook will tell you that good management involves motivating your staff. Motivation develops as a direct result of feeling valued and confident in the job – having the skills and knowing the routines. Assistants feel valued when they are included as part of the learning support team and accepted as part of the school staff. There are still some schools, in the minority thank goodness, who treat their assistants as second-class citizens – e.g. not allowing assistants in the staff room! You can do a lot to make assistants feel confident and creative by providing opportunities for sharing the planning process described in the next section. LSA attendance at annual reviews and case conferences has been very helpful when the contribution has been planned with the SENCO beforehand. This sort of involvement leads to a more committed and motivated staff.

Teachers now undergo regular appraisal as part of their work. In line with this practice, as SENCO you could develop an annual performance review for the assistants in your school. This can provide an opportunity for celebrating their success as well as giving improvement suggestions and constructive criticism. As a two-way process, it will also give the assistants the chance to share their views about how to improve arrangements.

Given regular opportunities for planning, discussion and evaluation with teacher colleagues

In 1992 a report by the Audit Commission/HMI was published. This was entitled *Getting in on the Act*. The report described the provision made by schools and LEAs in England and Wales for pupils with special educational needs and made recommendations for action at national and local levels to improve the effectiveness of this service. The management handbook *Getting the Act Together* was published as a companion volume. This document provides detailed guidance to schools and LEAs and in it there is a section (Chapter 10) about managing extra adults in the classroom. There are several action points recommended to schools and teachers but the main recommendation is: schools and teachers should plan the use of extra adult support for pupils with special needs. Where extra adult help is provided, planning and communication are the key to improving its impact.

We don't really need telling this – it is sound common sense and yet it still does not happen enough in our schools. We need to make *time* for planning, we need to make *time* to ensure that our paper plans (much helped now through advice on how to complete IEPs) are *communicated* to those LSAs who will implement the plans and as a result become real and effective. As SENCO you will need to negotiate this with the other members of staff and help them to understand the importance of such planning. Discussions with both teachers and LSAs highlight the importance of time spent together in order to plan, monitor and evaluate Individual Education Plans. These meetings should be on at least a weekly basis and, in some cases, on a daily basis. If, as SENCO, you feel that not enough or even no time is allocated for this purpose, then it is clearly an issue which you should be addressing with the head teacher and with the other members of staff in your school.

How can this planning time be used effectively?

The IEP forms a sound base for discussion. As SENCO you will need to give some thought to whether it is better to meet with individual LSAs or teachers to discuss individual cases or whether small groups can gain from each other's experience – there is probably a place for both ways of working, depending on the child's needs. There is one particular principle to be recommended when reviewing the arrangements for each child and evaluating effectiveness – 'If it works, do more of it. If it doesn't work, do something different.' You need to set clear, achievable objectives involving the child and the LSA in this process if possible. This forms the basis of a useful plan. The next step is to consider how best to put the plan into practice.

Clear about the learning objectives

This point follows on well from the previous one. Consider this analogy – if you were setting out on a journey you would plan a route and a destination. If you didn't know where you were going or how to get there you would become confused, frustrated and angry and the journey would take much longer. Just as for a journey you need a destination and a route, so for a child to learn effectively the adult delivering the learning programme must know the 'destination', i.e. the learning objectives and the best route. This will mean developing an awareness of the learning style of the pupil – whether they learn best through visual, auditory or tactile cues, or a combination. And just as the time of day the journey is taken might affect the route and the time it takes, so for a learning programme the supporting adult should be sensitive to the best time of day for effective intervention. This is particularly important with younger children, e.g. a learning support assistant implementing a speech and language programme will probably find the child more receptive to a short session early on in the school day.

Clear about the learning and emotional implications of the child's special need

Each type of special need has associated implications for learning and it is important that the assistant is aware of these implications so that realistic learning objectives can be set, e.g. a child who has specific learning difficulties is likely to have great difficulty in copying from the board; a child with cerebral palsy is likely to have perceptual difficulties.

All children want to belong to the wider group. As SENCO your role will be to help assistants recognise when a child is settled and happy and to understand that emotional factors can override the learning plan. LSAs should be encouraged to work in such a way as to downplay any differences and encourage inclusion as much as possible. Judging how the child works best, whether in class or out of class in small groups, is an important task. The child must feel settled before learning can take place.

Often it is not too difficult to say *what* needs to be done for a child; *how* it is to be done will be more problematic. As SENCO this will be the issue which will require creativity, sensitivity and detailed communication to the LSAs and teachers with whom you work.

Deployed efficiently, effectively and flexibly

In an article for *Special Children* (May 1992) entitled 'Help or hindrance' Margaret Balshaw describes a scenario in which lack of communication and planning result in a less than helpful experience, not just for the child, but for the parent too, mainly as a result of the over-dependence of the child on the assistant, the over-involvement of the assistant together with the lack of involvement of the class teacher and the assistant taking on the role of 'teacher substitute'. What this leads to is a child who becomes more isolated rather than more included – the work of the assistant is in fact counter-productive. It might have been much better had the assistant been more flexible in the approach and been advised to work within a group context, in this case moving in to work individually with the child only when absolutely necessary.

Things can go wrong if assistance is badly managed. Your IEPs might be perfect but unless they are able to be put into practice they remain just pieces of paper. So in your role as SENCO, how can you ensure that assistance is used efficiently, effectively and flexibly to bring the plan to life? The report referred to earlier, *Getting the Act Together,* provides some answers.

Advice to teachers

Three action points are recommended to teachers.

Teacher and supporting adult have agreed in which lessons there is a role for the latter.

You should decide in which lessons the LSA really needs to be giving support to the pupil and in which lessons he or she might usefully be employed elsewhere. To quote from the handbook:

> It is not uncommon for a supporting adult to sit through a lesson with virtually no useful role because the style of the lesson precludes working with individual pupils. Examples of this are class discussions and use of audio-visual resources. With a degree of planning, the supporting adult need not spend the whole time in the lesson.

An instance is described in which a supporting adult for a child with visual impairment was not in the classroom, but usefully preparing Braille worksheets elsewhere, once it had been checked that the pupil could manage in this lesson without support – and this was a practical science lesson in which assistance might be assumed to be vital! Common sense is clearly needed in negotiating the best use of special needs assistance.

It is good practice for the LSA to work with the pupil in the mainstream classroom whenever possible. Consideration should be given as to whether the LSA should work alongside the pupil, with a small group of pupils or at a distance observing when the pupil needs support, and moving in only at those times. The LSA should be encouraged to promote the independence of the pupil at every possible opportunity.

Role of the supporting adult has been planned.

It is essential that the teacher spends time clarifying relative roles and responsibilities. It is clear from the work done with LSAs and teachers that time spent in planning is time very well spent. 'If a small amount of the time currently spent alongside pupils were redirected into planning and discussion about individual pupils between support (supporting adults) and classroom teachers, there would be a *significant improvement* in effectiveness.' Moreover, both teacher and LSA would feel better about their work with pupils who need learning support, and the pupils would reap the benefits of partnership working.

Teacher or supporting adult prepares special materials if necessary. To increase pupils' independence, consideration is given to preparing special lesson materials as well as providing side-by-side support.

It is likely that the pupil or pupils supported by a learning support assistant will need worksheets and activities which are modified in some way so that he or she can understand the instructions and complete the task with some degree of success. This is particularly the case if the pupil has learning difficulties. Given clear directions by the teacher, the LSA can be of great help in providing these special materials. This point recognises the importance of allowing the pupil to work independently rather than having an assistant sitting alongside all the time. A 'beneficial circle' is described, in which 'professional time is used to modify resources which enable the pupil to exercise more independence, thus freeing further professional time'.

In considering how best to use assistance, it is also of vital importance to consider the views of the child. This is especially true for older children who can clearly say what they would prefer. In secondary schools, students seem to hold one of two views. Firstly, there are those who like nothing better than to have additional support in subjects they find hard and are quite happy for this to be given in a class setting, often preferring that the assistant is seen working with others at times or with small groups. Secondly, there are other students who absolutely hate being singled out as being different in any way from the rest of the group.

CHECKLIST FOR ACTION – MANAGING EXTRA ADULTS IN THE CLASSROOM

Action by teachers	Action by schools	Already in place?	Action required?
Teacher and supporting adult have agreed in which lessons there is a role for the latter			
Role of the supporting adult has been planned			
Teacher or supporting adult prepares special materials if necessary To increase pupils' independence, con-sideration is given to preparing special lesson materials as well as providing side-by-side support			
	Time is allocated for communication between teacher and supporting supporting adult		
	School managers observe impact of extra adults in classroom on pupils with special needs		

(Source: Audit Commission/HMI.
Getting the Act Together, HMSO)

Conformity and belonging to the group is so crucial for most adolescents that anything which can lead to derision by others is rejected. This issue spans a number of areas (dress, hairstyle, eating habits, etc. – ask any parent!) Be aware of these issues which relate to belonging and self-esteem and endeavour to use assistance sensitively. Sometimes working outside the main group (out of sight, out of mind) enables the young person to relax and this provides a better learning context.

If, as SENCO, you can facilitate the effective use of LSAs it will certainly lead to a wider range of activities for pupils, better differentiation according to ability, and teamwork in the classroom.

Efficient? Effective? Flexible?

In some cases, there can be more than one additional adult in the classroom and this presents the teacher with a more complex management task. Support from the SENCO is needed in discussing the 'how to' in this case. What is necessary here is a well-planned but flexible negotiation of adult roles, and advance planning is crucial. One observed Year 7 group of 20 students had four adults in the classroom – one teacher, one support teacher for a child with hearing impairment and two assistants to support students with behavioural difficulties. This was not an efficient, effective or flexible lesson mainly because the class teacher did not assume authority over the group and the students did not seem to know just where the authority was vested. There had obviously been no planning. With some forward planning, this lesson would have been very much better. For any lesson with more than just the class teacher, the adults need to agree beforehand:

- What are the learning objectives for this lesson?
- Who will assume overall authority, introduce the lesson and delegate the tasks?
- Who will work with whom?
- Who will be responsible for resources?
- What particular strengths each will bring to benefit individuals/the group and at what time in the lesson this will be appropriate?
- When will the assistant(s) intervene and when will they observe?
- How to use differentiated material depending on the range of abilities in the group.
- What to do if a child becomes disruptive.

Given opportunities for training and development

One of the most consistent messages coming from learning support assistants who have had no training is that they lack confidence in what they do. This can be inhibiting and prevents participation and creativity. It is a particular problem for assistants who are newly appointed and unsure of their role. The need for providing encouragement and training is clear if confidence is to be boosted.

Certainly, assistants learn a great deal by watching good teachers at work. As SENCO, you might consider formalising a system of teachers as mentors, especially for newly appointed assistants.

In an effective working partnership, the teacher will take every opportunity to develop the knowledge and skills of the learning support assistant within the normal working environment and in regular meetings. It will also be very helpful to the development of the LSA if he or she can be encouraged to attend any relevant in-service training courses. It can also be useful for assistants to visit other schools in order to observe good practice and discuss common issues with other LSAs. This is particularly helpful in a small school which has only one or two LSAs, when sometimes the role can seem rather lonely and practice can become 'stale'. Often, new development opportunities can rekindle enthusiasm and bring new ideas. (More details of training needs and training routes are described in Chapter 8.)

The resources of your learning support assistants can make a significant difference to the school experience of a child with special educational needs if used to best effect. If, as SENCO, you take time to ensure LSAs are clear about their job – what to do, when to do it and how to work – and to provide training to develop their skills, these investments will result in a more effective learning experience for the child and a motivated and committed team of assistants.

CHAPTER 5

The role of the class teacher in working with the learning support assistant

In your school, the special needs coordinator (SENCO) is likely to have the responsibility for managing the overall workload of the LSAs. However, as much LSA time is spent in class, working alongside class teachers, it is important to consider how best the assistant and the teacher can work together. The class teacher has a key role to play in managing the work of the LSA. It is the teacher's job to direct children's work in all lessons and to negotiate the role of the assistant in delivering the curriculum to the class. This negotiation about what part the assistant will play can be discussed with the SENCO and depends to some extent on the individual education plans for the children requiring learning support.

Teachers who work with learning support assistants identify the following aspects of their role:

How can the class teacher support the LSA?

- ensuring the LSA is clear about his or her responsibilities in the classroom;
- providing regular opportunities for planning and discussion;
- encouraging the work of the LSA and providing positive feedback;
- making sure the LSA knows the learning support implications of the pupil's special need;
- making clear and realistic requests;
- valuing the LSA as part of the learning support 'team'.

Ensuring that the learning support assistant is clear about his or her responsibilities in the classroom

When teachers start their first teaching appointment, it is after considerable time has been spent in training and teaching practice. However, the majority of LSAs have not had any training when they start work and their experience of school life may well be limited to their own school days. So, a learning support assistant who is new to the job will need a period of induction when 'on the job' training will be required. The LSA is unlikely to understand the frameworks within which schools operate and will need help in understanding a wide range of issues from, for instance, the process and content of the National Curriculum to how to share a book with a child. In practical subjects the assistant will need to be shown how to use equipment correctly and to understand safety procedures.

It is very important and helpful to both the teacher and the assistant if the ground rules for working together are negotiated at the start of each school year (see Chapter 2, 'What are the ground rules?'). This is more of a task in secondary schools where assistants have more teachers to work with. Some secondary schools now allocate assistants to departments so there is more familiarity with both staff and the curriculum. This is not possible, of course, when assistance is linked to individual pupils.

Providing regular opportunities for planning and discussion

The importance of regular meetings for planning, monitoring and evaluating the work of the LSA is vital and is the key to ensuring a high quality learning experience for the pupil who needs learning support. Ideally, the teacher, the assistant and the SENCO will have regular meetings every so often in order to do this – this is often built into reviewing IEPs. On a daily or weekly basis however, the teacher and assistant need to negotiate who does what in the lesson. The teacher will certainly need to consider how best to use the assistant. This could be in working with an individual child, or with a small group. Or again it could be preparing appropriate worksheets or equipment for the children who need additional support. The question of how to use assistance efficiently, effectively and flexibly is discussed in more detail in Chapter 4.

Encouraging the work of the LSA and providing positive feedback

Most LSAs, particularly when new to the role, admit to feeling under-confident about their work. This is usually because they have been away from the workplace for some time and also because they have had no training about what to expect, either in terms of the role they will fulfil or about the special needs they will meet. Encouragement from teachers is important in order to build confidence. Positive feedback about what has worked well and constructive criticism provided as 'improvement suggestions' can work wonders in transforming unsure LSAs into enthusiastic and confident colleagues.

Making sure the LSA knows the learning support implications of the pupil's special need

Each type of special need has associated implications for learning support. It is important that the teacher explains these implications to the learning support assistant so that realistic outcomes can be expected from the learning tasks. For instance, a pupil with emotional problems may achieve very little academically on some days. On such occasions a 'listening ear' may do much more in supporting the pupil than will insistence on the completion of a page of writing.

Knowing the learning implications entails providing work for the pupil at the right level so that success is likely (differentiation). It is important that the teacher makes clear to the LSA just what the purpose of the learning task is so that alternatives can be considered if necessary.

Making clear and realistic requests

When asked about issues which prevent effective partnership working, LSAs report that they are sometimes asked to do tasks which they feel they cannot do, either because they are unclear about the task or because they feel they do not have the expertise. As a teacher, therefore, do not assume that the LSA has psychic powers but make requests clear, checking that the LSA has understood. Encourage the assistant to ask if they are unclear. Remember that it is the responsibility of the teacher to decide the teaching methods, the materials to be used and the recording system. It is also the responsibility of the teacher to manage and monitor the work of the LSA in the classroom. This can only be done effectively if communication is clear and realistic and if the LSA is not overburdened with responsibilities which clearly belong with the teacher.

Valuing the LSA as part of the learning support 'team'

It is important that the learning support assistant is encouraged to see himself or herself as part of a 'team' in supporting pupils with special needs. The class teacher can encourage this perception by valuing the views of the assistant and ensuring that the perspective of the LSA is shared whenever there is a full case discussion about the pupil. This may be as part of the Annual Review process or at a case conference. The class teacher has a role in encouraging other members of staff and also the parents to have a positive view of the learning support assistant as a colleague who works in partnership with teachers and parents to meet children's needs.

Margaret Balshaw in her book *Help in the Classroom* (1991) describes several scenarios when things go wrong for the assistant as a result of the teacher's mis-management of the situation. Four such scenarios are as follows:

The overgrown pupil

This is when the assistant is ignored in terms of his or her support role and treated almost as though he or she were another child in the group. As a teacher, you should be aware of the role the assistant can play and assistants must beware of acting like an 'overgrown' pupil.

Piggy in the middle

This is when the assistant feels like the 'go-between' and happens when the teacher assumes that the responsibility for the pupil lies solely with the assistant. The assistant finds himself or herself overburdened and unsupported. It also happens when the teacher gives an activity for the assistant to carry out with the child or group of children and, not long into the activity, the assistant realises that the task is not 'matched' to the children and feels awkward in having to report back. These difficulties can be avoided by joint planning and good communication. The SENCO has a part to play here in making clear the respective responsibilities of the teacher and the assistant and facilitating planning time.

Spy in the classroom

This is when the teacher may feel that the assistant is in some way 'spying' on him or her and there is a resulting mistrust between the adults involved. It is important that adults work together to support children and that any personal difficulties can be ironed out. This can be done by involving a third party, e.g. the SENCO.

Dogsbody

This is when the assistant is used by the teacher in a way which is perceived as unfair. There have been occasions when teachers have used assistants to escort disruptive pupils from the classroom and 'mind' them for some time. This may very occasionally be appropriate, if this has been negotiated beforehand or if the assistant is employed to work with a particular pupil who is disruptive but it is a problem raised by a number of assistants. Using an assistant as a classroom 'skivvy' is also unacceptable. They will generally be very pleased to help clear up but clearing up should be recognised as the responsibility of pupils and teachers too.

It must be said that these scenarios are the exception rather than the rule, although it is clear from work done with assistants that their view of their roles and responsibilities is not always the same as that of the teacher.

The following activity may be useful in establishing common ground. It is for both teachers and LSAs to complete separately, then to compare notes to identify any mismatch. It then can guide discussion about how best to support each other.

You are a teacher/an assistant (ring as appropriate).

Please read the following statements and give a rating to each statement:

The LSA you work with is: OR As an LSA I am:	not at all	not much	just OK	pretty much	very much
• clear about roles and responsibilities	1	2	3	4	5
• valued as part of the learning support team	1	2	3	4	5
• given regular opportunities for planning with teacher colleagues	1	2	3	4	5
• clear about learning objectives	1	2	3	4	5
• deployed efficiently, effectively, flexibly	1	2	3	4	5
• given opportunities for training and development	1	2	3	4	5

Now compare your ratings with the teacher/LSA you work with and discuss which areas can be improved for you both and how you might work better together.

CHAPTER 6

What special needs will I be supporting?

How do children learn?

In starting to think about learning support, it is important for all adults who work with children to understand the ways in which *all* children learn.

The following principles, put together by Hampshire Inspection and Advisory Support Service (1992) are fundamental statements about learning and are true for all children, whether they are described as having special educational needs or not.

WAYS IN WHICH CHILDREN LEARN

- Children learn primarily through practical and first-hand experiences.
- Children learn through all of their senses (with the rare exceptions of children who have severe sensory impairment).
- Children make sense of new experiences by relating them to previous learning.
- Children develop their understanding through talking.
- Children have different preferred learning styles and learn at different rates.
- Children may move across subject boundaries as they learn.
- Children learn best when they can make sense of what they do through involvement in planning and reflections.
- Children learn through purposeful repetition, practice and reinforcement.
- Children learn best when there is care, tolerance, security, praise and high expectations, associated with clear learning goals.

We hear a lot about children's 'learning difficulties' and the current framework means that some children are categorised as having mild, moderate, specific or severe learning difficulties.

It is important to view learning difficulties as a relative term.

Remember: 'If the tasks and activities in which the learning is engaged are not matched to the learner's capabilities, or are not understood by the learner, then learning difficulties are likely to occur' (Ainscow and Tweddle 1988).

The importance of matching the task to the child is made very clear in the 1981 Act. This stresses that 'special educational needs' is a relative term which arises from the interaction between a child and his or her environment. By planning realistic and achievable learning tasks, learning difficulties can be avoided. As a learning support assistant you are there to work with the teacher to remove the 'barriers' to learning.

Imagine that you are given a pair of knitting needles, a large ball of wool and a complex knitting pattern. Imagine too that you are in a group who all have the same task, which is to knit, say, a cardigan pocket in one hour. What would be your reaction to the task? I would predict that a very small minority of you could do this; for the rest, perhaps some would try as best they could, managing a few rows or more. But I would anticipate that the majority of you would give up after a short time and the reasons for this might be many and various, e.g.

What stops children from learning?

- you can't knit;
- you can knit but only follow simple patterns;
- you can't read;
- you haven't got your glasses so can't read the instructions;
- you are German and the pattern is written in English;
- you have broken your arm so have only the use of one hand;
- you can't see the point of knitting this particular garment;
- you don't like the colour;
- you are allergic to wool next to the skin;
- no-one is available to help you when you are stuck and to encourage your feeble efforts.

We need to ask a question here about how in fact we might indeed learn to be successful in knitting the pocket. That question is 'What needs to happen in order for you to do this task successfully?' The answers will vary depending on what stopped you from learning in the first place.

I would suggest that we start by assuming you can all do the task given the right conditions and support. Let's take the 'learning difficulties' and consider how to remove the barriers to learning.

Knitting task

Learning difficulty	*Needed to be successful?*
- you can't knit	- someone to teach you how to knit
- you can only knit simple things	- someone to give you advanced knitting lessons
- you can't read	- someone to teach you how to read
- you haven't got your glasses	- bring them next time
- you can't read English	- have the pattern translated into German
- you only have use of one hand	- wait until other hand is better or learn to use a knitting machine

- you can't see the point of knitting this garment
- you don't like the colour
- you are allergic to wool
- no-one is available to help you

- find something you can see the point of knitting
- change the colour
- choose a synthetic yarn
- find someone who can teach and encourage you

The task would take more time for some of you than for others and you may need specialised teaching or equipment to be successful. In addition, you would certainly be affected by the performance of other people in the group. Imagine how you would feel if you were sitting beside someone who had no difficulties and who had completed the task in the time limit. It might make you feel badly about not 'keeping up' and could damage your self-confidence, making you want to give up and go home. You might even start distracting others out of boredom!

This example can help us in understanding the difficulties some children face when presented with tasks which are beyond them. It helps us to see why some do indeed give up and start to feel like failures. We need to work so that children experience success and that comes by ensuring that we anticipate the barriers to learning and remove them, providing the task *at the right level* so that success is probable.

We need to know:

- what level the child is at so the next small step can be planned and taught;
- what equipment might help learning, e.g. computer programme for encouraging reading, a sloping desk surface to aid writing position, etc.
- what the child's preferred learning style is, e.g. whether he or she prefers visual or auditory input or both together;
- what pace the child learns at;
- how much teaching repetition and practice is needed;
- when is the best time of day for certain types of learning to take place;
- where the child is likely to learn best, e.g. in small groups or whole-class work;
- how much the child is encouraged or discouraged by the children around him or her;
- how much encouragement the child needs from the teacher and the assistant.

As teachers and assistants we must always be ready to change or modify the task so that the child *can* learn. This is often done 'on the hoof' but can be discussed when reviewing the IEP, and remember:

- realistic objectives should be set – be clear about the capabilities of the child and don't expect too much, or too little!
- learning activities should be matched to the ability of the child so success is assured;
- learning should be planned in small steps with frequent repetition – go over what has been taught often so that the child does not forget;
- a wide variety of materials and opportunities to learn through first-hand experiences is necessary – learning through doing;
- give plenty of encouragement – children thrive on praise.

When we think of learning in this way, the proposals for moving children currently in special schools into local mainstream schools can be realised, given the right levels of support. Schools often feel unable to support disabled children, yet children with and without disabilities have much in common. If 'learning support' based on individual and group needs is put at the heart of school development planning and the school aims to tackle the full range of needs then this can improve the learning environment for everybody.

> It is evident that every child will gain from an inclusive approach. All children can feel comfortable and supported as an inclusive approach recognises every one of us has a variety of abilities. Growing up as friends with people who may look or sound very different means losing fears and unfamiliarity which turn into prejudice. The inclusive approach will lead to children developing into adults who are able to accept and value difference.
>
> (Rieser 1994)

In your work as an assistant it is important that you are aware of the wider perceptions of people in society about children who are viewed as different and that you work to encourage an understanding and acceptance of difference as part of ordinary life.

Do we need special provision?

'They wouldn't give us these labels if they had to wear them afterwards'

As the special educational needs/Code of Practice framework currently stands, there are different kinds of special need described which may require additional learning support.

These are:

- mild learning difficulties;
- moderate learning difficulties;
- specific learning difficulties (dyslexia);
- dyspraxia;
- severe learning difficulties;
- profound and multiple learning difficulties;
- physical disability;
- sensory impairment (visual or hearing);
- language impairment;
- communication impairment including autism and Asperger's syndrome (Autistic Spectrum Disorders);
- emotional and behavioural difficulties (including AD/HD – Attention Deficit/Hyperactivity Disorder).

It is important that this categorisation is not viewed negatively and used to fit children into particular 'boxes' which then determine expectations and segregated provision but that each child is seen as a human being with his or her learning needs which can be addressed successfully given the matched learning programme.

Mild learning difficulties

It has been estimated that 18 per cent of all pupils will have some kind of mild learning difficulty at some time during their school life. These pupils are unlikely to have a statement of special educational need. Learning support assistants are frequently called upon to support such pupils whose mild special needs may be described as follows:

- mild conductive hearing loss (e.g. 'glue ear');
- slight physical disability (e.g. mild cerebral palsy);
- poor eye/hand coordination;
- clumsiness;
- hyperactivity;
- slow to develop reading and writing skills;
- general immaturity;
- poor vocabulary;
- slow to understand new ideas;
- short concentration span/distractibility.

These pupils should not need a high level of support but attention needs to be given to particular areas of need with the possibility of including structured activities to support the particular need.

The vast majority of children who have mild learning difficulties lack self-confidence in their learning ability. Please remember to take every opportunity to enable the child to succeed and be ready to give praise and encouragement for small amounts of progress. What appears to be a small step may be a giant leap for the child.

Moderate learning difficulties

Pupils described as having moderate learning difficulties are often those pupils who have limited ability in both verbal and non-verbal skills. They are pupils who learn at a slower pace than do other boys and girls of the same age.

It used to be the case that these children were educated in special schools. Since the 1981 Education Act and its emphasis on children being educated in the mainstream where possible, increasing numbers of 'mld' pupils have their needs met in ordinary schools, usually with additional teacher support and/or learning support assistance. The main indicator of whether this is in the best interests of the pupil is the ability of the pupil to cope with the social and emotional demands of a mainstream school setting, and the ability of the mainstream school to provide an appropriate curriculum and welcoming ethos. There may remain a number of 'mld' pupils who require the more sheltered and nurturing support which special schools offer and who would struggle to cope and fail to thrive in a mainstream setting. It may be possible to replicate more 'sheltered and nurturing' environments in mainstream schools given the resources to do this.

Pupils who have moderate learning difficulties often have the following associated problems:

- poor memory;
- short attention span;
- slow progress in literacy and numeracy skills;
- limited ability to apply learning in one situation to another situation (generalisation);
- inability to understand abstract ideas.

If you are working with a child who is described as having moderate learning difficulties, please remember:

- *He or she needs practical work in order to learn* ('active learning').
  Every opportunity for using visual aids and practical apparatus should be used.

- *Overlearning is necessary.*
  Frequent repetition and practice of skills acquired is important in order to reinforce learning.

- *Language work is essential.*
  Vocabulary and language use is likely to be poor, so regular activities which broaden vocabulary and increase understanding of language are essential.

- *Progress in literacy and numeracy will be slow.*
  The class teacher and SENCO will help you to understand how best to support children learn to read, spell, write and do maths work.

- *Confidence building is crucial.*
  Children described as having moderate learning difficulties often have low self-esteem and perceive themselves as failures, so take every opportunity to give praise and build confidence.

- *Life skills will need to be taught.*
  Young people who are described as having moderate learning difficulties need help to learn those skills for living they will need when they leave school, e.g. filling in forms, managing their money, relationship issues etc.

Severe learning difficulties

Pupils described as having severe learning difficulties usually are those pupils who have very limited general ability and who learn at a much slower pace than do other boys and girls of the same age. These learning difficulties are often because these children are genetically different from most other children (e.g. Down's Syndrome) or because of medical trauma (e.g. brain damage as a result of tumour or oxygen deprivation at birth).

Most of these pupils are educated in special schools although some are wholly or partially integrated in mainstream schools and the future will see more of these children being educated in their local mainstream schools with the teaching resources they require.

Pupils who are described as having severe learning difficulties have similar characteristics to those with moderate difficulties but they frequently need a higher level of adult support and learn at a slower rate. Even as adults, some may be unable to cope independently without the support of caring adults. It is therefore necessary to teach life skills (shopping, cooking) to these pupils as a priority, particularly as they get older. The younger child will take longer to learn 'self-help' skills (e.g. feeding, use of toilet) and your help is likely in these areas.

If you are working with a child who has severe learning difficulties, please remember:

- *Slow progress is likely.*
  Progress may be slow but the children can and do learn given consistent support at the right level.

- *Practical experiences are vital.*
  The need for 'first-hand' experience is clear (e.g. shopping trips to learn about the use of money).

- *Language work is essential.*
  Encouraging understanding of language and use of language is very important in the learning process.

- *Allow the pupil to choose.*
  Try to provide the pupil with opportunities to make choices, as it is by developing the ability to choose that control over the environment is developed. Don't let the pupil become too dependent on you!

Profound and multiple learning difficulties

Pupils described as having profound and multiple learning difficulties have both severe physical disabilities and severe learning difficulties. They may also have sensory impairment (hearing and sight). These children often have limited understanding of language and little or no speech, so communication is often difficult.

When working with these children, most of whom are currently educated in special schools, the first priority must be their physical comfort. There will be many routine tasks (feeding, dressing, toileting) which these children cannot do for themselves and your help will be required. In order to assist with some of these tasks you will need clear directions on how to move pupils from one place to another, for both their benefit and your own.

Backache is a common complaint among adults who work with children. Do ask about how you can avoid this and learn the correct techniques for lifting and moving children.

Once the child is comfortable, the priorities then become educational. Establishing some means of communication is of key importance. This may be through visual contact, through touch, through sounds, through taste and smell, i.e. working through all the senses.

If you are working with a child who has profound and multiple learning difficulties, please remember:

- These children can and do learn although progress is often very slow.
- Try to understand what messages the child's behaviour may be communicating.
- Have positive expectations.
- Give encouragement and praise even though you may be unsure of whether the child understands. Assume that he or she does! If you seem to get no response, it may be because the child cannot physically make the response – there may be an emotional response which you cannot see.
- In some cases, children will actually regress as a result of medical factors and occasionally a child may die. Be aware that this is a possibility.

Specific learning difficulties (also called dyslexia)

Pupils described as having specific learning difficulties have average general ability but poor literacy skills (reading, spelling, writing) and sometimes poor numeracy skills. There is a mis-match between the pupil's ability to understand and answer questions verbally, which is good, and the ability of the pupil to read, spell or write, which is poor. These sorts of problems are sometimes referred to as dyslexic difficulties. A significant number of children have specific learning difficulties which are relatively mild and more boys than girls are affected. A small number (maybe one or two in each school) have quite marked difficulties requiring a high level of support.

These pupils usually have limited ability to remember letter shape and sequence. They often have what is described as 'phonological difficulties', which is the ability to manipulate the sounds of letters into words. They can benefit from what is known as a 'multi-sensory' approach to learning. This means using visual, auditory and kinaesthetic (movement) strategies or clues to help them learn and remember which letter sounds and letter shapes go together. The SENCO and class teacher can help you understand how best to support children in learning to read, spell, write and do number work.

If you are working with children who have specific learning difficulties, please remember:

- Find out what the child is good at and make sure those skills are valued. Pupils who have specific learning difficulties frequently experience feelings of frustration and loss of confidence so it is important that self-esteem is boosted.
- The child is not being lazy if he or she seems to have forgotten all the work done at the last session – or even five minutes ago! Strategies for remembering sequences and written information are poor so daily activities to improve memory can be of great value.

- Copying from the board or from textbooks may be very difficult. Give the child small photocopied chunks at a time or read the words to him or her and give support in encouraging writing.
- Allow the child to use a Dictaphone to record ideas, e.g. in creative writing or describing a science experiment. You may then be able to transcribe the words which the child can then copy.
- Encourage the use of a word-processor for recording information. The Spellchecker facility can really help to boost the confidence of these children.
- These children often have trouble remembering sequences, e.g. months of the year. Their sense of direction is often poor. Make allowances for this and give practical activities wherever possible.

Dyspraxia

Dyspraxia is a label given to marked difficulties in coordination. It is described as an immaturity in the organisation of movement and may also affect language, perception and thought. A useful description is: 'Problems in getting our bodies to do what we want when we want them to do it.' (Ripley, Daines and Barrett 1997).

The Dyspraxia Foundation estimates that it affects at least 2 per cent of the population in varying degrees and 70 per cent of those affected are male.

Children described as dyspraxic are often described as 'clumsy'. They bump into things and fall over more often than most children and they have difficulty learning to do tasks which involve a high level of co-ordination such as getting dressed, writing and riding a bike.

What signs might indicate 'dyspraxic' difficulties?

The Dyspraxia Foundation lists the following possible indications of difficulty:

- clumsiness;
- poor posture, poor body awareness and awkward movement;
- confusion over handedness;
- sensitive to touch and find some clothes uncomfortable;
- poor short-term memory – can forget tasks learned that day;
- reading/writing difficulties – holding of pens can be awkward;
- poor sense of direction;
- finds it hard to catch, run, skip or use equipment;
- immature behaviour;
- poor organisational skills;
- activities requiring a sequence are difficult, e.g. maths or any subject requiring a series of tasks;
- poor awareness of time;
- easily tired;
- lack of awareness of potential danger, especially important in practical and science subjects.

Before the teacher and LSA plan an IEP for the child it is important to observe the child, paying attention to the following areas:

- Gross motor skills – observation in PE will reveal if the child is having more difficulty than most in following action sequences. If the child takes ages to change for PE this may also indicate coordination problems.
- Fine motor skills – observing how the child responds to art and craft activities (using scissors, rulers, etc.) will reveal any problem areas.
- Speech – listen to the child's pronunciation. If it is poor and the child mixes up words or sounds, then this may indicate a problem.
- Perceptual skills – observe how the child matches patterns or copies sequences of words, letters or numbers – if he or she takes ages or gets it wrong then there will be a need for support.
- Literacy and numeracy – watch how the child responds to the teacher, sets out written work and see whether he or she works logically. If the work is very untidy and poorly presented or there has been only patchy understanding then there will be a need for support.

How can I offer support?

Children described as dyspraxic usually are of average intelligence and their verbal communication can often be good. When working with a child described as dyspraxic it is important to remember the following guidelines:

- Break the learning task down into small steps so that each step can be mastered before moving on to the next step in the sequence.
- Practise these small steps daily, e.g. in buttoning a shirt you may need to start by showing the child where to put his fingers and how to hold the button.
- Provide written lists, e.g. the timetable, equipment necessary for particular lessons and attach these to the child's school-bag using luggage labels.
- Do not expect the child to copy large chunks of information from the board.
- Encourage use of word processors/laptops/palm tops for recording written information.
- Ask for information given by the teacher to be repeated by the child (perception checking).
- Remember to boost the self-esteem of the child by recognising success and encouraging him or her in doing anything they can do well, e.g. singing, helping others, conversing etc.

Occupational therapists can be asked to help in some cases and can work with the child in order to recommend particular equipment or approaches. Where difficulties severely affect a child's progress in school, referral to the occupational therapist for further assessment is advisable. The occupational therapist may treat the child's problems directly and/or set up a programme in school (with advice to the family at home). Such programmes are often carried out by the LSA who is trained by the occupational therapist to work with the individual child; monitoring and review are carried out on a regular basis. Advice on management and equipment will also be given.

A useful book giving more information about Dyspraxia is *Dyspraxia, a Guide for Teachers and Parents* by Kate Ripley, Bob Daines and Jenny Barrett (David Fulton Publishers).

Physical disability (pd)

The term physical disability covers a wide range of conditions. The more common ones you are likely to come across include:

- cerebral palsy
- spina bifida
- hydrocephalus
- cystic fibrosis
- muscular dystrophy
- diabetes
- epilepsy
- haemophilia
- limb deficiency
- asthma
- brittle bone disease
- eczema

Within each category, the effects of the disability range from the relatively minor, so that the child can lead a 'normal' independent life, to relatively severe, so that the child cannot function without the support of caring adults.

Until quite recently, pupils with physical disabilities attended special schools but ideas about physical disabilities have changed from the rather negative concept of 'handicap' to the more positive concepts of 'disability' or 'impairment'. The rights of people with disabilities to have access to normal experience has been recognised and the general public is much more aware of people with disabilities and the part they play in community life. Now, whenever possible, these pupils should have their needs met in mainstream schools. There are still a considerable number of these children whose additional needs are such that special schooling is appropriate at present. These are the ones whose health is often at risk, who require very specialised equipment or who require daily intensive physiotherapy, i.e. those who would 'fail to thrive' in a mainstream setting either physically or emotionally, but the future will see more of these children being educated in their local mainstream schools with the resources there to support them.

Different disabilities result in different learning support needs. You will need to ask the teacher you work with about the details of the disability – educational psychologists, teacher advisers and school medical officers (doctors) can also give you details of associated learning difficulties and physical needs. For instance, pupils who have cerebral palsy sometimes have visuo-perceptual difficulties, i.e. they do not perceive visual images in the same way as other children. Pupils with hydrocephalus sometimes have mood swings and times when they feel very tired. Pupils with spina bifida sometimes have poor fine motor control (i.e. poor control of pencil and hand movements).

On the other hand, it is likely that pupils with e.g. cystic fibrosis, asthma or brittle bone disease may have no learning difficulties as such but they may need a sensitivity to other needs, e.g. tiredness, mood swings, and assistance in managing equipment or physiotherapy routines.

One step behind

Promoting independence is an essential part of your role with all pupils who need learning support. It is particularly important for pupils who have physical disabilities. You need to be 'one step behind' rather than 'one step ahead'. This means allowing the pupil to take calculated risks, on occasion – you will need to discuss this with the class teacher, head teacher, teacher adviser and on occasions the school medical officer, and think through the possible consequences!

It is a difficult task to maintain the balance between giving support and promoting independence. This involves you being clear about your expectations and firm in your directions without pressurising the child. However, sensitivity should tell you if and when to intervene.

Self-help

Part of your role may be enabling the child to look after himself or herself and to master those skills which able-bodied children take for granted, e.g. feeding, dressing, going to the toilet. When helping children in these ways it is important to treat them with dignity and respect and to provide privacy when appropriate.

Mobility

Pupils may need aids in the form of wheelchairs, crutches, mechanical limbs or calipers in order to get around. You will need to familiarise yourself with this equipment and make sure the pupil can use it with comfort and control. Most children learn to transfer themselves from place to place when required, e.g. from a wheelchair to the toilet, with little help. Younger children or very disabled pupils may need more help. If you need to assist in moving a child, you must know the correct techniques for lifting in order to avoid injury to either yourself or the child. Ask for support – quite literally! Lifting techniques must be taught, for each child, by a physiotherapist.

When working with a child with a physical disability, please remember:

- Behave towards him or her as you would to any other pupil of the same age.
- Do not do all the talking for the child or answer for him or her. Let the child make choices so he or she feels they have some control of their environment rather than becoming a passive recipient of support. Give him or her the *time* to make a response – these children often take longer to respond. Often their thinking response is immediate but controlling arms and legs, voice or equipment to aid communication can take time.
- Make sure you know the implications of the disability (physical, educational and emotional).

Further useful information about supporting children with physical disabilities can be found in a booklet entitled *Working Together Towards Independence* (Fenton 1992).

Sensory impairment, as the name suggests, refers to any impairment of the senses which may prevent normal progress and development. There are two main types, visual impairment (VI) and hearing impairment (HI). Rarely, children will have both.

Sensory impairment

Visual impairment (VI)

A survey by the Royal National Institute for the Blind indicates that in Britain there are approximately 10,000 children aged 2 to 19 years who have visual impairment as a primary disabling factor. If children with visual impairment and additional special needs (e.g. profound and multiple learning difficulties) are considered, then there are at least double that number.

This survey also showed the increase over recent years in the proportion of VI children who go to mainstream schools, with varying levels of support, a lot of this support coming from learning support assistants together with peripatetic teachers of the visually impaired.

The impairment may be moderate, in which case your work might be mainly concerned with adapting materials and ensuring safety. If the impairment is severe you may need to learn Braille and keyboard skills in order to produce materials the child can use and thus learn effectively. You may also need to assist the child in learning how to get around the classroom and the school with safety. It is important to understand the limits of the child's vision.

When working with a visually impaired pupil, your responsibilities are likely to be as follows:

- to provide support for the class teacher by adapting teaching materials, e.g. enlarging worksheets, so that the pupil can follow the same programmes of work as the other members of the class;
- you may be asked to supervise the specialist equipment and resources, e.g. magnifying equipment;
- to ensure the safety of the pupil and others, e.g. safe use of science equipment;
- to support the pupil by helping him or her to learn any special skills, e.g. Braille.

You will need to offer support in all areas in which he or she may be disadvantaged. These areas are:

Orientation and mobility

Clear verbal directions are necessary before any task involving physical movement is attempted. The visually impaired child may not have a visual image of what is required so a visual demonstration is a waste of time, e.g. in PE, if the class teacher is demonstrating, you may need to talk through the steps, for instance, 'Move three steps to the right, jump with both feet together, then three steps to the left'.

Environmental awareness

Visually impaired children must be helped to become aware of their surroundings and learn how to cope with a range of situations both inside and outside.

Games and leisure

It is sometimes difficult for children with sight problems to join in with informal games and conversations. You may be able to help here, by opening up possibilities for the child you work with to join in and become part of the group.

Social skills

The child with a visual impairment has a social communication problem as he or she cannot always see and therefore interpret the intentions of others. A major way in which children learn is through copying other children and adults but a child with a visual impairment may be unable to do this. This means that he or she will be unable to see a great many actions, facial expressions and non-verbal messages and, as a result, may miss out on this type of learning. Don't be offended if these children use the wrong non-verbal messages and be prepared to teach them the acceptable ways of interacting in a group situation (e.g. remind the child to turn his or her face towards you when speaking). Some playground supervision may be necessary and your role might be to encourage inclusion of the child in group activities as far as possible.

And remember:

Visually impaired children often miss out on ideas and meanings because of limited vision. It is therefore important to use 'hands on' experience whenever possible, e.g. when talking about leaves, give the child some leaves to hold or, better still, take the child to a park and let him or her feel a tree and walk through fallen leaves to hear the noise that makes.

For more information the following books are useful:

A Blind Child in my Classroom by Gillian Gale and Peter Cronin, Burwood Educational Series RNIB.

Supporting Children with Visual Impairment in Mainstream Schools, INPUT.

Hearing impairment (HI)

There is a wide range of hearing impairment, from mild to profound, although total lack of hearing is extremely rare. Statistics published by the National Deaf Children's Society estimate that there are 28,000 school-age children with significant hearing impairment. 14 per cent are educated in special schools for the deaf, 15 per cent in units attached to mainstream schools, and 71 per cent are in their local mainstream schools. More children are likely to be educated in their local schools in future. Many of these children receive support from a peripatetic teacher of the hearing impaired. Assistants support these children by working with the class teacher and following specialist advice which allows the pupil to play as full a part as possible in school life.

Children who have normal hearing skills acquire ideas and concepts about the world around them largely through spoken language. The words we use to describe objects and experiences provide the child with a 'framework' to build on and learn effectively through reasoning and memory skills. For the child with a hearing impairment, understanding of language is limited, so this 'framework' which is vital for learning is incomplete. These children may then appear slow to learn, particularly in language-based tasks of speaking, listening, reading and writing. Reasoning and memory skills may also appear to be poor. However, many of these pupils have normal ability and good non-verbal and visual skills and most acquire spoken language in the same way as hearing children but at a slower rate. There are many factors which influence whether a hearing impaired child hears and understands speech. These include:

- the kind and degree of hearing loss;
- the age at which deafness developed;
- the age at which it was discovered;
- the issue and proper use of a suitable hearing-aid;
- early training;
- attentiveness of the child.

(Bennett 1985)

As a learning support assistant working with the child you may find it helpful to be clear about these factors in the child's background in order to understand the hearing loss and its educational implications. Ask the specialist teacher of the hearing impaired to discuss this with you.

If you support a child with a hearing impairment then you need to appreciate that the child has a *communication* problem and that your first task is to ensure as far as possible that the child is reliably receiving and understanding all communication from staff and pupils and is routinely participating in all class activities. Your role with the child who has a moderate to profound loss might involve ensuring the correct use of any hearing-aid equipment provided for the child, and you may also need to learn a signing system if that is advised as appropriate for the child, although relatively few children use signing in mainstream schools.

Your role with the child who has a hearing loss will involve ensuring that the child is in the best position in the class to hear what the teacher says and checking with the child, by asking, what they have understood about the task they have to do.

When working with a child with hearing impairment, please remember:

- The sense of hearing is limited so reinforce as much spoken language as possible through the other senses. Visual clues through lip-reading, signing or natural gesture may be necessary to ensure that the child understands. You can be advised about this by a teacher of the hearing impaired.
- Pupils with moderate to profound hearing loss may be unable to acquire the skills of speaking, listening, reading and writing at a normal rate. For these children it is essential to provide individual programmes to focus on the development of these skills. For these children appropriate activities and/or modifications to the curriculum may be advised by a specialist teacher who will discuss your role in implementing these with you and the class teacher.

- Use visual aids and real experiences whenever you can.
- Communicating with others is a basic need. Pupils with hearing impairment may feel frustrated about their inability to communicate and so may lack self-esteem and occasionally become aggressive. You will need to establish communication with the child yourself, and help others to do so. You may also need to be particularly sensitive to the child's emotional needs.
- Rephrase, reiterate and extend your language whenever possible to give the hearing impaired child a better understanding of difficult concepts. Be creative!
- Be aware of social isolation and endeavour to foster friendships and inclusion of the child with the peer group.
- Hearing-aids and radio systems are the child's link with the sounds around him or her. Learn how the systems work and how to monitor the development of listening skills.

For further advice

If you want to know more about hearing impairment then the following resources are useful:

Understanding Childhood Deafness (1996) by Wilhma Rae Quinn, Harper Collins.

Supporting Children with Hearing Impairment in Mainstream Schools, INPUT.

Spotlight on Special Educational Needs – Hearing Impairment (1996) by Linda Watson, NASEN.

Language impairment

It has been estimated that there are approximately 250,000 children under five and the same number between 5 and 16 in England and Wales who have language impairment. Some are in special schools but the majority attend mainstream schools (figures from the Association For All Speech Impaired Children, AFASIC). If identified at a pre-school level, these children receive support from speech and language therapy services and a fortunate few attend nurseries with specially trained teachers and therapists. For some children appropriate support in those vital early years is enough to enable them to overcome their difficulties but others go into school with an 'invisible' disability and require ongoing support from teachers, speech and language therapists and learning support assistants. Often the role of the LSA is to work with the child to follow an individual programme which is monitored by the speech and language therapist and the teacher. This is likely to require a short time each day working individually or in small groups with the child. It will be helpful if you can look for ways of practising individual work in classroom activities.

The term 'language impairment' covers a range of difficulties. It is helpful to think of these difficulties in the following ways:

Difficulties in understanding (receptive language)

- limited knowledge of vocabulary;
- difficulties in understanding meanings of words.

Difficulties in speaking (expressive language)

- range of uses for which language is employed;
- poor pronunciation;
- disordered structure of language (words omitted, in the wrong order, tense, etc.);
- limited vocabulary;
- stammering.

Different types of difficulty require different intervention. There are many children in our schools who have delayed language development (i.e. language develops normally but at a slower rate) and who benefit from language 'enrichment' activities. This means providing new experiences and teaching the words to use alongside these experiences. Other children have disordered patterns of language development and these pupils require a more intensive approach, using the skills of speech and language therapists and specialised schemes (e.g. the Derbyshire Language Scheme, Makaton sign system, Blissymbols, Picture Exchange Communication System (PECS)).

If you are working with a child who has a language impairment, it is important that you and the class teacher meet with the speech and language therapist to discuss the child's particular difficulties and how you can provide effective help. The programme can form part of the individual education plan (IEP).

Here are some guidelines for working with language impaired children:

- Get the child's attention before interaction. Often listening and watching are required by the child to help understanding.
- Main content words should be stressed and understanding will be helped by exaggerated intonation.
- Use simple signs or natural gestures to help the child understand your message.
- Use short, clear sentences.
- Talk about objects and activities in which the child shows an interest.
- Talk about actions as they are happening.
- Give the child *time* to respond. Responding in turn is a valuable skill, so try not to dominate the interaction.
- Encourage all spontaneous utterances where appropriate and help the child to feel an equal partner in conversation.
- Do not ask too many questions because they may discourage communication. Balance your talking with comment and description as well. Make up simple 'stories' using favourite toys.
- Use expansion and extension of the child's utterances.
  Expansion – repeat the sentence adding words that were missed out.
  Extension – a reply that broadens the focus of attention.
- If sounds or words are said incorrectly by the child, repeat the

utterance yourself to show the correct way to say it. This is valuable feedback and should sound natural rather than like a 'correction'.

- Don't try to correct everything at once. Choose a sound, or a concept, to focus on for a week or two.
- No-one enjoys being corrected all the time. We all learn best when we feel relaxed, confident and are enjoying the task. Therefore, praise the child when his or her speech is clear, new words are attempted, or longer sentences are tried.
- Encourage the child to express him or herself through art and craft work or construction toys.

For further information see *Spotlight on Special Educational Needs – Speech and Language Difficulties* (1996) by Daines, Fleming and Miller, NASEN.

Communication impairment (Autism/Asperger's syndrome)

Many pupils with special needs have difficulties communicating effectively as a result of a learning difficulty or physical or sensory impairment. However, there are a small number of pupils whose major problem is an inability to communicate with and make sense of the world around them. These children have normal physical appearance and can hear and see but they fail to understand meanings of language and of social situations. Some of them seem to lack the desire to communicate socially. Children having this kind of difficulty sometimes have a medical diagnosis of autism, or if they are more able, of Asperger's syndrome (Autistic Spectrum Disorders).

These pupils are relatively rare and most of them are educated in special schools. More able pupils can cope with mainstream schools, when supported by learning support assistants.

Some of the special characteristics associated with this difficulty are described as follows:

- limited ability to interpret the social cues in any interaction, e.g. the emotions of the listener;
- poor at modifying tone of voice and content of language to 'match' the other half of the conversation;
- limited understanding of jokes and ironic content of language;
- poor play skills or use of imagination;
- stereotyped behaviour or routines (e.g. rocking, twiddling hair, hand flapping);
- literal interpretation of language (e.g. '*pull your socks up*');
- anxiety.

As a result these pupils need to be taught social and communication skills. If you are working with a child who has a communication impairment, please remember:

- These children frequently take things literally and this can cause anxiety. It is therefore very important to explain statements and instructions carefully using words, actions, pictures or role-play to help the child's understanding of the situation. Sometimes the child may have unfounded but genuine fears about certain objects, animals or people. Some may dislike the noise and disorder of playtimes. You need to be sympathetic if this happens and help the child to cope.

- These children need help to know *how* to behave in social situations. Your role might be to show them what is expected and to encourage appropriate behaviour.
- These children tend to withdraw when they cannot make sense of what is going on. You may need to *anticipate* what will cause anxiety and make changes accordingly. It is very helpful if you can prepare the child for what is going to happen next, by talking him or her through the situation, particularly if it is a new experience for the child.
- Physical activity (e.g. jogging, ball play) can be helpful in reducing anxiety and physical tension. Music and relaxation techniques will help.
- Do give praise and encouragement. Even though it may not seem to be received, these children need positive feedback and reassurance.
- Be careful in your use of facial expression. Some children get anxious if they feel you are cross with them, this may result in difficult behaviour.

More information about children with communication impairment can be found in: *A Mind of One's Own*, a guide to the special difficulties and needs of the more able person with autism, for parents, professionals and people with autism. (Digby Tantam, The National Autistic Society).

Supporting children with literacy difficulties

Many children with special educational needs find difficulty in developing literacy skills. In your work as a learning support assistant you may be asked to help children in these areas of work. As part of the National Primary Strategy most schools for children in the primary age range now have a 'Literacy Hour' each day. The daily hour is split into four sections. The first section is whole class work, sharing a big book or a shared passage. The second section is a whole class session on words or sentences. The third section is small group work on directed activities and there is a short session at the end for reporting back and planning.

Your role in this hour should be planned by the teacher you work with but is likely to include:

- Encouraging children to look and listen.
- Sitting close to children who find it hard to concentrate.
- Clarifying or repeating instructions or tasks.
- Working with a group on activities planned by the teacher.
- Reporting back to the teacher if the child is experiencing difficulties.

Encouraging reading

When sharing a book with a child do remember:

- An encouraging manner is vital to the child's success.
- These children often have poor memories so activities designed to develop memory skills are important.
- Use techniques which encourage success, e.g. you read most of a sentence leaving some words to be read by the child.
- If a child gets a word wrong NEVER say 'no'. Correct by saying 'This word is . . . Can you say it now?'
- Allow some mistakes if this does not stop the general flow of reading.
- Make it fun for younger children by hiding a page that has just been read and asking quiz questions about the meaning or the pictures.

Encouraging spelling

Many teachers use simple techniques of LOOK/COVER/WRITE/ CHECK to help children in learning spelling. This is just as it sounds:

LOOK – The child looks at the word – saying it aloud will also help as will tracing over the letter shapes with a finger.
COVER – The word is covered up.
WRITE – The child tries to write the word from memory.
CHECK – The child checks whether the word is right and tries again if not.

There are many software programmes which help children to improve spelling skills which are now available to schools.

Encouraging writing

Many children are disheartened when it comes to putting pen to paper because it is difficult for them. When helping the child do remember:

- Encourage any effort the child makes on his or her own.
- Check that the child is sitting and holding the pen correctly.
- Some children find it difficult to copy from the board. You may need to transcribe work onto paper for copying.
- Some children find it easier to record work using a word processor, especially children who find it hard to write neatly. Do encourage this whenever possible as it is often more motivating for children.

Supporting children who have numeracy difficulties

Some children described as having special educational needs require additional support to develop numeracy skills – the skills of understanding concepts of size, shape, relationships and number. Many find it difficult to do mental arithmetic or simple computation tasks. The DfES has issued guidance to schools about teaching numeracy as part of the Primary Strategy for schools at the primary stage. As for literacy, there is a daily lesson on numeracy which includes regular exercises in mental arithmetic, problem solving and teaching of new skills. Whole class work and small group support are part of this structure. There are additional modules to support slower learners. Assistants often deliver these modules.

Encouraging numeracy

When working with a child who has numeracy difficulties do remember:

- The basic language of maths needs to be taught and understood.
- The child need to learn concepts of size, shape and classification as basic building blocks to understanding.
- Learning using practical apparatus and equipment is necessary for many children.
- Children who have poor memory skills will need practice and repetition.

There are also a number of good software programmes now available which children find attractive and which help them to learn.

Fox and Halliwell (2000) and Halliwell (2003) offer more advice on giving support.

CHAPTER 7

Supporting children with emotional and behavioural difficulties

In the course of your work as an assistant you will come across a considerable number of children who need support because of emotional or behavioural difficulties. The 1981 Act recognises that emotional and behavioural needs are special *educational* needs because no child can learn optimally if they are unsettled or unhappy in school for whatever reason. Sometimes these difficulties are caused as a result of physical, sensory or learning disability but often they are rooted in difficult home backgrounds. There is usually a combination of factors which come together to cause the child to exhibit signs of emotional or behavioural difficulty. In a recent study of pupils considered to be 'at risk' of exclusion from their secondary schools, all had recent or current traumas in their home life; 75 per cent had poor reading skills and 25 per cent were identified as having quite marked signs of mental health problems (bulimia, fire-setting etc.).

Emotional and behavioural difficulties is a blanket term which includes a very wide range of conditions – perhaps the only characteristic these share in common is that the children experiencing them are both troubled and troubling to those who come into contact with them.

What do we mean by emotional and behavioural difficulties?

The emotional difficulties which lead to interpersonal and social problems range from, on the one hand, 'internalising' behaviour, e.g. withdrawal/shyness, depression, extreme anxiety and compulsions, to 'acting out' behaviours (sometimes called conduct disorders), e.g. extreme aggression (to people or property), anti-social behaviour, bullying, defiance.

If a child receives inadequate emotional nurturing from the parents or carers, particularly at an early age, then the likelihood of emotional and behavioural difficulties is high. Physical and sexual abuse also increase the likelihood of emotional and behavioural difficulties.

Learning difficulties can also cause emotional problems for children. A sensitive educational environment and *curriculum* at the right level is necessary.

There are many factors which indicate difficulties of this kind and the vast majority of children, at some point in their school lives, will have some emotional and behavioural problems – indeed it is part of normal development. Children with special needs of any kind experience these difficulties as part of their perception of themselves as being 'different'. However, it is when problems persist over a long period of time and become severe and complex that additional support will be necessary.

Pupils experiencing severe emotional and behavioural difficulties may need special provision where small class groups and a high level of adult attention is offered. There are many pupils in our mainstream schools who also show these difficulties and schools report increasing numbers of such pupils. Learning support assistants play a significant part in supporting them and making it possible for them to remain in their local schools. The majority of these children do not achieve what they are capable of in academic subjects at school because no child can learn effectively if he or she is troubled inside and has feelings of worthlessness.

What 'problem' behaviours will I see in the classroom?

In your work as an assistant you will become aware of a range of 'problem' behaviours in the classroom. These will range from mild 'low-level' disruptions to full-blown tantrums or defiance. Assistants who work with these children have noted the following behaviours as those causing concern:

- pencil-tapping;
- humming;
- kicking the table legs;
- chair-rocking;
- out of seat a lot (can't sit still);
- poking, pushing, 'interfering' with others;
- shouting out;
- constant talking, giggling;
- taking others' equipment;
- lashing out at others;
- swearing or shouting;
- defiance;
- throwing equipment;
- damaging equipment or property;
- spitting;
- bullying;
- withdrawn behaviour;
- frequent crying;
- running away;
- hiding;
- stealing.

It is important to note that most classrooms are well-managed by teachers and most behaviour problems are of the 'low-level' type. It is rare to have major outbursts or fighting in class and if or when it does happen it is the responsibility of the teacher to react appropriately. If you are working with a particularly difficult child then you need to sit down with the teacher and plan just who will do what if a major problem should occur.

In order to prevent problems occurring and to stop escalation of incidents it is important to do some analysis of just what causes the difficult behaviour in the first place. Of course, you cannot do anything about the child's home life but you may be able to identify when a 'difficult' day is in prospect by judging the mood of the child first thing in the morning. In this case you will need all your best 'active listening' skills to encourage the child to talk about what might be troubling them. You may be able to provide some quiet time away from the class group for the child or young person to 'settle' before going into lessons.

You can also prevent difficulties arising in the first place by following some of these suggestions:

- sit the child next to a well-behaved pupil – sitting him or her next to a 'sworn enemy' is a recipe for disaster;
- ensure he or she is sitting near the front of the class with few obstacles to pass on the way to his or her seat;
- ensure the child has all the equipment he or she needs;
- give the child tasks and activities which he or she can do – too difficult a task can cause frustration which may lead to disruptive behaviour;
- give the child 'positive' attention early on in the day. Children who are 'attention-needing' are going to get your attention one way or another – usually this is through the 'negative' attention of being 'told off'. However, if you are pro-active in this process and give praise and good messages to the child *before* things start to go wrong, then you are more likely to prevent difficulties arising.

Some key ideas in supporting children who have emotional or behavioural difficulties

(See also Chapter 3, Giving Support – 'How can I support the pupil?')

Take every opportunity to improve the self-esteem of the pupil

Give praise when they conform to normally expected standards of behaviour in school or when they have achieved something they have never done before. This can be related to school work or to behaviour. Try to 'catch them being good' and let them know why you are pleased.

'Jenny, I like the way you came into the classroom this morning.' (behaviour)

'Robert, you've read those words really well today. Well done!' (school work)

All children seek to belong to the group and their self-esteem can be badly damaged if they are excluded by other members of the class. As an assistant you need to foster peer group acceptance of the child so that he or she is not left out.

Rewards are very important

This shows the child when he or she is succeeding and that it is worthwhile to succeed! Find out what your child values as a reward. Sometimes a word of praise or a pat on the back can be enough but for many children described as having emotional and behavioural difficulties

this will not be enough and you will need to provide more tangible rewards (a wall chart with targets, a favourite game etc.).

Develop your listening skills (see 'Supporting the pupil', Chapter 3)

You will be sensitive to the feelings of the pupil if you can listen and observe effectively. If you can encourage the pupil to talk about feelings, it can be helpful. Try to look for solutions to the problems rather than dwelling on the causes. (Ask 'What needs to happen in order to avoid this situation in the future?'). There will be many parts of the pupil's life which you cannot change for the better. Accept this and concentrate on those parts you can change (e.g. self-esteem, patterns of behaviour in school).

Encourage the pupil to take responsibility

Many pupils with emotional and behavioural difficulties find it very hard to take responsibility for their own actions. Enabling them to understand what effects their behaviour has on others is an important step in moving towards changing unhelpful behaviour patterns. Role-play or drama activities can be very helpful to these pupils in enabling them to do this.

If you can give the pupil a position of responsibility in the group then this will also assist the development of mutual support and social responsibility and it will also foster a sense of trust.

Point out good role models

Do not assume that the child knows how to behave. You may need to teach him or her the behaviour which is needed in school. If you can demonstrate yourself what is wanted or get the child to copy another child who is behaving well then you will be demonstrating what is expected. Do not overdo this however – it can be very bad for self-esteem if it is always being pointed out that others do it right!

Try to anticipate trouble

Learn to recognise those situations in which problems for the pupil commonly arise, e.g. lining up at the door, coming in from break, being late for lessons. Help the pupil to recognise these situations for himself or herself and work out strategies for minimising or avoiding trouble. If a pupil can learn to keep out of the way of other pupils who seek confrontation, then this can make a tremendous difference to his or her life in school.

Deal with 'bad' behaviour in a positive way

By the very nature of their difficulties, these children will not always behave like the majority of the others and their anxiety or anger will 'spill over' in school. However, when incidents or confrontations do occur, it is important to deal with them in a calm and reasonable way. Remember to label the behaviour and not the child. Calling a child 'stupid', 'naughty', 'bully', 'slow' only serves to reinforce the idea in the child's mind that they are indeed 'stupid', 'naughty', 'bully' or 'slow'. The message must be 'I like you but I don't like your behaviour'. It is often helpful to talk about the effects the behaviour has had and the feelings it engenders in others: 'Jane, when you take money from the teacher's drawer it lets me down, and I'm sad about that because I want to trust you.'

Communicating your own feelings about the incident can be helpful: 'John, I feel angry when you mess about because you don't give me your best work and I know you can do better than this.'

Staying calm is very important. If you 'lose your cool' it will only serve to make the pupil feel worse and increase the likelihood of the incident occurring again.

Be realistic

Be realistic in setting goals for the pupil. Don't try to change all 'bad' behaviour at once. Choose one objective to start with (e.g. sitting in seat for five minutes, not shouting out for ten minutes). Be consistent, make it clear to the pupil what you are aiming for and reward the pupil if the target is achieved. Remember that it took a long time for the pupil to learn their patterns of behaviour, and overnight transformations are unlikely.

Helpful information and workshop activities for improving self-esteem in children can be found in a video workshop pack 'A Bag of Tricks' (Barbara Maines and George Robinson). There is a useful booklet to accompany the course, *You can – you know you can*, Lucky Duck Publications. This may be accessible through the school's educational psychologist.

You will need to work with the teacher in order to develop an IEP (or IBP – individual behaviour plan) for the child. You may be asked to do an observation of the child in a particular lesson in order to find out exactly where the problems are coming from. The following framework provides a structure for deciding how to support the child. It works best

Planning to support children with behavioural difficulties

if you can make this plan together with the class teacher and if you *both* carry it out.

Planning a structured behavioural programme for an individual child

There are a number of points to bear in mind when planning a behavioural programme.

It should be:

Workable   – makes sense to you and the child with clear targets. It will work best if all adults who work with the pupil are clear about the plan (teachers, parents, LSAs).

Achievable – you should plan it so that the child is successful.

Realistic   – don't try to change all 'bad' behaviour at once. Start with one thing and work in steps towards success. It should be the right thing for the pupil in the situation, e.g. choosing 'staying in seat' when other children are moving round is not realistic.

Manageable – it should be easy for you to monitor and record results.

Step one

Write a short list of those behaviours you want to reduce. Next to these behaviours write the ones you want to see instead, e.g.

Unwanted behaviours	Desired behaviours
Shouting out	Listening/working quietly
Getting out of seat	Staying in seat

Step two

Do an observation of the child. Become a 'fly on the wall' for half an hour and watch what is going on. Make a chart so that you can record what is happening. This will give you baseline information and provide a starting point. Here is an example of an observation chart:

OBSERVATION SHEET

Name: _____

Lesson: _____   Time of day: _____

	shouts out	out of seat	'on task'
10.00 – 10.05	3	2	3 mins
10.05 – 10.10	2	0	2 mins
10.10 – 10.15	2	1	1 min
10.15 – 10.20	0	0	0 mins
10.20 – 10.25	0	1	4 mins
10.25 – 10.30	2	2	2 mins
TOTAL	9	6	12/30

From this observation it would make sense to target shouting out as a priority. You may want to share these results with the pupil to agree you are aiming for a zero score but in the first week it might be more realistic to go for e.g. six – whatever reduction seems realistic and actionable. You would then explain to the pupil that the behaviour you want is 'keeping quiet in lesson time and raise hand to speak'.

Step three

Review your list in step one. You may have noticed other behaviours which become priorities. Decide which particular behaviour you want to encourage, e.g. staying in seat, keeping hands to self, staying quiet and putting hand up to say something.

Step four – environment analysis

Now look at what you might do to prevent this behaviour occurring in the first place. Consider whether you can change the location, peer group, subject, activity in order to eliminate or reduce the unwanted behaviour. For example:

If a pupil always gets into trouble when seated next to another particular pupil then don't allow them to sit together.
If a pupil starts distracting others shortly after a task has begun, ensure the task is clear and achievable when it is given.
If a pupil finds it hard to get started on a task, ensure he/she has all equipment necessary before you start.
Can any of the following be changed to prevent the behaviour happening in the first place?

Can these be changed?	YES	NO	HOW? and WHO?
Location of pupil (e.g. proximity to teacher)			
Location of pupil (sitting beside whom?)			
Subject lesson			
Task			
LSA			
Teacher (e.g. parallel groups)			
Child's physical state			
Child's emotional state			

Step five – teach new skills

Children need to be taught how to behave. You may need to demonstrate appropriate behaviour by role-play or by pointing out others modelling the right behaviour. The child may need considerable practice. Role reversal where you play the part of the child, and the child the teacher can increase perception! For example:

'This is how I want you to come into the classroom.' (demonstrate)

'I want you to keep your hands together on the table when I'm speaking.' (demonstrate)

'I like the way John has started work straight away. I want you to do that.'

'I want you to keep quiet when I'm talking and put your hand up when you want to say something.'

Step six

Share the results of your observation with the pupil. Explain that you are going to work together to encourage e.g. 'staying in seat' by cutting down the times he or she is out of his or her seat. Ask the pupil what needs to happen in order for them to stay in their seat. Involve the pupil in setting a target for the next similar lesson, i.e. cut down from eight times to four times out of seat. Monitor and check how things are going – 'How's it going?' 'You're doing well.' 'You're remembering to sit in your seat. Well done.'

Other possibilities

Problem behaviour	Target behaviour (positively phrased)
Shouting out	Keep quiet and raise hand to speak
Out of seat	Stay in seat
Distracting others by poking	Keep hands, feet and objects to yourself
Seeking a great deal of adult attention	Work alone for five mins

Step seven – positive reinforcement of appropriate behaviour

Negotiate a reward for meeting the target (make the target easy to achieve). Ask the pupil what he or she would like as a reward. Suggest one if he or she doesn't come up with anything realistic. Suggestions for rewards would be:

Infant/Junior
Bubble blowing
Decorating plain biscuits with icing and sprinkles
Extra time on the computer
A favourite game
Music while you work
Certificate to take home to parents
Special responsibility

Secondary
Extra computer time
Pen
Keyring
Certificate to take home
Cooking
Special responsibility
Free ticket to school disco

The lottery principle

It is sometimes even more motivating if several rewards are possible, each written on a card and put in an envelope. One 'reward' should be extra special. The pupil takes a chance on choosing a reward and might get the 'star prize'.

Step eight

If the target is achieved give reward and praise and record on a chart for the pupil to see. Set a new target for next similar lesson, e.g. twice out of seat.

If the target is not achieved, make it easier and say 'We'll try again tomorrow'.

Step nine

Continue for two weeks giving the negotiated reward for targets which are achieved. Review the programme. Continue to make targets clear and to teach any new behavioural skills the child needs and review environmental factors.

Step ten

Do another observation and compare it with the original. Use the same lesson and same time of day. Is there any improvement? If not, why not? Consider appropriateness of task, peer group and environment.

Step eleven

Choose another behaviour, e.g. 'Now that you're able to stay in your seat most of the time, we're going to choose another target. What do you think we could work on next?'

Remember to keep a written or picture record of what is achieved. The pupil might enjoy doing this themselves, e.g. putting stickers on a chart. Negotiate a 'super reward' for the pupil after two weeks of improvement. Send any good news home to share with parents.

Ensure the task the pupil is given is at the right level for his or her ability. Problems often occur when pupils are bored or the task is too hard.

Step twelve – reactive strategy

If you have provided an optimum environment for the pupil, e.g. task at right level, sitting by non-troublemakers and the pupil deliberately chooses not to follow an instruction then you will need to discuss with the teacher what sanction to apply. The first 'reactive strategy' should be a warning, e.g. 'If you keep on getting up out of your seat, you will be moved away from the group.' Children dislike being moved to sit away from their friends so this is quite an effective 'mild' sanction. This should only be done for short periods at a time. Evidence suggests that it is not the severity of the sanction but the consistency with which it is applied that makes the difference.

Attention Deficit/Hyperactivity Disorder

Attention Deficit/Hyperactivity Disorder (AD/HD) is a label given to a certain set of behaviours, some of which are the same as those behaviours observed in children described as having emotional and behavioural difficulties.

AD/HD is more 'behavioural' than 'emotional' and is thought to be caused by the biological make up of the child, having its roots in neurology, whereas most emotional and behavioural difficulties are thought to be a 'normal' reaction of the child to adverse external influences.

For AD/HD, three main factors are described:

1. inability to control impulses;
2. inability to focus attention for any length of time;
3. inability to control motor activity (in some cases).

AD/HD is a medical diagnosis and the drug Ritalin is often prescribed in order to help the child to concentrate and so to help him or her to settle to learn in school. As part of your work as an assistant, one of your jobs might be to monitor the behaviour of the child who is taking Ritalin, working with the teacher and the school nurse. Many adults who work with children are uncomfortable about controlling the behaviour of children using drugs and there is a view that too many children are identified as having AD/HD and sometimes it may seem like 'the medicalisation of social difficulties'.

It is important to manage these children in similar ways to other children with behavioural problems so all the advice given in the previous section is relevant. In fact it is important to plan 'behaviour modification programmes' and to judge their outcomes *before* drugs are prescribed although this sometimes does not happen.

Useful references for more detailed information about behaviour management are:

Attention Deficit/Hyperactivity Disorder: A Practical Guide for Teachers (1997) by Paul Cooper and Katherine Ideus, David Fulton Publishers;

Practical Strategies for Individual Behaviour Difficulties (1997) by Geraldine Mitchell, David Fulton Publishers;

Supporting Children with Behaviour Difficulties: A Guide for Assistants in Schools (2001) by Glenys Fox, David Fulton Publishers;

Supporting Children with Special Educational Needs (2003) by Marian Halliwell, David Fulton Publishers.

CHAPTER 8

The special needs of learning support assistants

You may be so busy fulfilling your support role with the pupil, the teacher and the school that you may overlook the fact that you yourself have special needs – the need for support, encouragement and for training.

The class teacher or SENCO with whom you work has a really important influence on whether you feel well-supported or not. Those parts of your work affected by this relationship are addressed in earlier chapters. Essentially, you need support to know what you have to do, how you need to do it and how successful you have been. It is sometimes quite easy to find out the 'what' and 'how' of a task but it is often quite difficult to know whether you have done a good job or not. Accept advice, know your limitations and those of the child, use your initiative to seek alternatives and ask for feedback on what you have done.

The need for support

You will feel well-supported if your school does the following:

- Provides you with a clear job description (see Appendix A).
- Uses your time well:
  - i.e. – not 9 – 10 a.m. then 2 – 3 p.m. on the same day.
  - not wasted sitting through whole school events when you could be preparing materials.
- Provides a permanent contract:
  - some LSAs are employed on temporary contracts and this is unsatisfactory. There will always be children in mainstream schools who need additional learning support.
- Provides adequate conditions of service:
  - even in these enlightened days there are still some assistants who are not allowed in the school staffrooms and some who have to do daily playground duties in their breaktimes.
- Provides career development opportunities:
  - through training, you might feel encouraged to do more courses and gain experience in working with different sorts of need – you might decide to go for additional qualifications. Some LSAs have been inspired to go on to train as teachers.
- Acts quickly to prevent confusion:
  - when problems or misunderstandings arise, it is important that the issues are dealt with speedily and with fairness.

In discussion with groups of assistants, it is clear that a number are confused about aspects of their work in schools. Much depends, of course, on the ability of the class teacher to appreciate how best to use assistance. There will be some systems and personalities in schools which are resistant to change, but there will always be *some* changes you can effect. In endeavouring to do this, you will need all those qualities described earlier in this book! ('What makes an effective LSA?'). Constructive criticism, couched in the form of 'improvement suggestions', will often be welcomed.

The following causes of confusion are frequently raised. Some possible solutions are offered:

CAUSES OF CONFUSION	HOW TO PREVENT CONFUSION
1. Lack of background information.	1. Ask questions. Look at school records.
2. No 'named' person to relate to or too many people telling you what to do.	2. Negotiate support from a nominated teacher.
3. Breakdown in communication.	3. Agree arbitrator to resolve difficulties/conflicts.
4. Lack of joint planning.	4. Request time for joint planning.
5. Lack of trust.	5. Encourage trust through consistent supportive work and readiness to work collaboratively.
6. Lack of support.	6. Form a support group with LSAs in your school or in neighbouring schools. Make your 'special needs' known to the special needs coordinator.
7. Unclear expectations of staff.	7. Planning, clear job description, clear timetable. Make staff aware of how you are able to work – the special needs coordinator can help you with this. Know your limitations. Use your strengths.
8. Unclear *how* to work with pupil.	8. Ask the teacher to demonstrate.
9. Unhelpful labelling, e.g. 'Mark's special lady helper'.	9. Negotiate your 'label' (see 'Groundrules', Chapter 2).
10. Assumptions made that the LSA has specialist knowledge.	10. Admit when you don't know; seek information.
11. No 'goals' set for the pupil.	11. Find out, by asking, what are realistic expectations and what objectives or goals should be set.
12. No training.	12. Ask to attend relevant in-service training. Visit other schools to share good practice.

From discussion with learning support assistants, it is clear that the job can be fulfilling, creative and rewarding. On the other hand it can be confusing, frustrating and demoralising. Most assistants seem to find themselves somewhere between these two extremes. When asked, the majority of teachers say how much they value the support and skills which LSAs offer, but there is one problem – they don't tell the LSAs that! Only a few schools provide constructive feedback on a regular basis to their assistants. This lack of encouragement from school staff is not deliberate but often happens. This is because, on the one hand, there is no space for evaluation of LSA input and also because teachers themselves do not receive enough positive feedback. (You can support the teacher by providing some of this!)

One of the most consistent messages coming from learning support assistants who have had no training is that they lack confidence in what they do. This can be very inhibiting and prevents participation and creativity. It is a particular problem for LSAs who are newly appointed and who are unsure of their role. The need for creating regular opportunities to review progress and provide encouragement is clear if confidence is to be boosted.

Teachers now have annual reviews or appraisal of their work. This sort of process could also be used for LSAs, allowing time for celebration of success and encouraging future projects.

The need for encouragement

The need for training

Why do we need training?

LSAs vary greatly in their background experience. A number are trained teachers who do not want the responsibility of a full class and full-time working. Some have no formal qualifications at all. Research by the National Foundation for Educational Research (NFER, Fletcher-Campbell) has shown that assistants range from ex-dinner ladies or parent volunteers who want more involvement with classroom life to people considering a career in teaching and who are exploring this by way of working as an assistant. Others are qualified teachers who wish to return to teaching following a career break and who see an assistant's role as a way of getting back into schools. All LSAs have experience of working with children either in school, e.g. as 'dinner ladies', or through voluntary agencies, e.g. Brownies, and the majority bring very important parenting skills to their role. This wide variation in background experience shows a clear need for training, especially since the role has become more educational with assistants being much more involved in the child's learning. The following scenario highlights this need:

> An assistant described a discussion between the class teacher, the parents of a child with special needs and herself. She was asked by the parents what particular training she had had in order for her to support their child and she had to say that she had no special training and had to rely on the guidance of the class teacher.

Parents need to know that their children are supported by people who know what they are doing. Schools need to be sure that children who need assistance are given informed and confident support from fully trained assistants.

Whatever their background experience, most assistants start the job with no specific training either about the role or about the special needs they might meet. Most assistants are now given some sort of in-service training once they have started the job, but also learn by 'trial and error' on a day-to-day basis and by watching teachers at work.

How can schools help?

As an assistant you can learn a great deal by watching good teachers at work. There are tried and tested ways of handling children which you can successfully copy. This works best if you ask for a particular skill to be demonstrated and talked through with you before and after the activity so that you are clear about how and why a particular approach works.

The SENCO probably carries the main responsibility for your day-to-day work. This responsibility should include 'on the job' training, with opportunities provided for planning and evaluation of what you do. Start by identifying together what you need to know and planning a programme to meet your needs. Ideally your staff supporter should be able to watch you at work in order to provide helpful suggestions. Of course, this can only work well when the teacher responsible is given time to do this – many school managers are now becoming aware of this need and are providing some space in the week to allow this to happen. Some schools are now asking teachers to act as mentors for assistants new to the job and in larger schools assistants form self-help groups. Training for LSAs is, in one sense, an ongoing process which takes place in the school on a 'drip-feed' basis as the teacher and LSA work together on a daily basis to determine ground rules, to plan programmes and to clarify responsibilities. The school has the responsibility for this aspect of training and as an assistant you have a responsibility to the child to ask when you are unclear about what is expected, e.g. you may be asked to work with a child using a computer and you may not know how to do this. Immediate training will be necessary.

Margaret Balshaw in her book *Help in the Classroom* gives useful advice and provides workshop materials for schools to use in school-based in-service training. These materials enable schools to make better use of classroom assistants. She suggests six principles of good practice for schools. These six principles are:

1. Classroom assistants should be clear about their roles and responsibilities.
2. Classroom assistants should understand the communication systems in the school.
3. Classroom assistants should be seen positively as part of the provision to meet children's needs.
4. Classroom assistants should be part of a working team.
5. Classroom assistants should be encouraged to make use of their personal skills.
6. Classroom assistants should be helped to develop their personal and professional needs alongside other members of staff.

Activities and scenarios are provided which encourage schools to look at each of these six principles in order to encourage partnership working and to plan more efficient and effective ways of using assistance.

Training in specific skills

There is clearly a need for specific training, e.g. if you are working with a pupil who has cerebral palsy you may need to learn certain physiotherapy routines, or if you work with a child who has a language impairment you will need to know what particular programme is relevant and why. In these cases the physiotherapist and speech therapist respectively will be the people who can train you (and the teacher) to use the right approaches. LSAs frequently ask for training in managing behaviour. The educational psychologist can give support in recommending ways of working with pupils who have emotional or behavioural difficulties.

Most LEAs have teams of advisory teachers who support children with special needs (e.g. visual impairment, hearing impairment, physical disability) and these teachers are able to support you with background information and practical advice.

Should there be a training qualification?

In the last few years a number of courses have led to qualifications for assistants. The difficulty here has been twofold – firstly, it has largely depended on geography as to whether assistants could access these courses and secondly, and perhaps more importantly, the quality of these courses has varied considerably.

It is now recognised to be in the interests of children for all LSAs to have training which is of high quality in terms of content and delivery. *Excellence for all Children* (DfEE 1997) states that:

LSAs' careers are being enhanced by a national structure including the following:

- national guidelines or a framework of good practice for LEAs and schools to follow;

- an expectation that LEAs will make available accredited training for all LSAs and oversee quality assurance;

- nationally devised modules of core training for teaching assistants;

- a range of accredited courses.

A framework of good practice, which has quality controls, is now emerging to provide LSAs, wherever they live, with a sound basis for working effectively and will formally recognise the contribution of assistants.

Aspects of training

There are several aspects of training:

- Training to understand roles and responsibilities (see Chapter 2);
- Training to understand the education and legislative framework (see Chapter 1);
- Training to understand general child development and how children learn (see Chapter 6);
- Training to understand specific skills needed to meet different learning support needs.

What should training include?

For all assistants it would be helpful to have a basic training which includes information about the following:

- respective roles and responsibilities of LSAs and teachers;
- legislation and current trends;
- Code of Practice and IEPs;
- background knowledge of the National Curriculum and ways of enabling access to that curriculum (including the National Literacy and Numeracy strategies);
- policies and procedures for SEN in the LEA and school (e.g. inclusion, SEN law, child protection etc.);

- support strategies;
- developmental aspects of learning – how children learn and what makes learning difficult for some children;
- managing pupil behaviour, motivating pupils, building self-esteem, problem-solving approaches, active listening;
- supporting the development of literacy skills;
- supporting the development of numeracy skills;
- supporting the development of language skills;
- use of resources including information and communication technology;
- assessing and recording children's progress and interpreting professional assessment.

Specialist modules for special educational needs

In addition to basic training needs, assistants will also need to access training to develop awareness, skills and strategies for supporting pupils with particular learning support needs in the following areas:

- literacy and numeracy (including dyslexia);
- speech and language, and signing;
- physical disability, motor coordination, sensorimotor and perceptual motor difficulty, including dyspraxia and cerebral palsy;
- hearing impairment;
- visual impairment;
- emotional and behavioural difficulties including AD/HD and challenging behaviour;
- autistic spectrum disorders;
- severe learning difficulties, including Down's Syndrome;
- medical difficulties, e.g. epilepsy, severe asthma, terminal deteriorating conditions and bereavement issues;
- social skills, communication, use of Circle Time;
- active listening and basic counselling skills;
- working with parents;
- working with support services.

Who can best deliver this training?

This training is ideally delivered by educational practitioners, i.e. educational psychologists, local authority SEN advisory teams and specialist teachers and SENCOs, as these are the people who are working very closely with children who need learning support.

Contributions of others for specific aspects of training will be beneficial, e.g. speech and language therapists, physiotherapists, occupational therapists, paediatricians, etc.

When should training take place?

In an ideal world LSAs would be trained before taking up appointment or as soon as possible once appointed. In-school 'informal' training, of course, starts on 'day one', but 'formal' training should be provided for all assistants as soon as it can be arranged.

National qualifications framework

At the time of writing, a new qualifications framework is emerging. This is based upon the recently published LGNTO National Occupational Standards (NOS) for Teaching Assistants. National Vocational Qualifications (NVQs) have been developed at Levels 2 and 3 in response to these Standards, and these two qualifications, together with DfES Induction Training, form the basic qualifications structure. There are many other qualifications available, some of which are similar in intention but which pre-date the NOS (e.g. City & Guilds Certificate in Learning Support 7321) and many more which were developed in order to extend LSAs' knowledge of teaching children with specific learning difficulties.

Teaching assistant qualifications accredited to the national qualifications framework in August 2002

Vocationally related qualifications	Occupational qualifications
CACHE Level 2 Certificate for Teaching Assistants NCFE Level 2 Certificate for Teaching Assistants Edexcel BTEC Level 2 Certificate for Teaching Assistants ABC Level 2 Certificate for Teaching Assistants NOCN Level 2 Intermediate Award for Teaching Assistants	NVQ Level 2 for Teaching Assistants (awarded by CACHE, OCR, City & Guilds and Edexcel)
CACHE Level 3 Certificate for Teaching Assistants Edexcel BTEC Level 3 Certificate for Teaching Assistants	NVQ Level 3 for Teaching Assistants (awarded by CACHE, OCR, City & Guilds and Edexcel)

What if a teaching assistant already has a qualification?

Many LSAs and teaching assistants come into the role from their experience of working with children in different contexts and may have achieved qualifications related to their previous experience. With the advent of the national qualifications framework, some awarding bodies are developing guidance on the accreditation of prior achievement (APA) to guide individuals who may have achieved qualifications some time ago and who want to update their skills. This guidance will help to show how earlier certificated achievements can be matched against the requirements of qualifications in the framework and, where appropriate, claim credit towards an accredited qualification.

What opportunities are there to progress to higher education qualifications?

Many teaching assistants and LSAs will have successfully completed a Specialist Teacher Assistant (STA) course and this can often be considered for credit towards a higher level qualification such as a Certificate of Higher Education, a Diploma of Higher Education or a foundation degree. As locally developed and delivered training programmes, different STA courses will be allocated different credit ratings. Some provide credit at further education (FE) level and would not be recognised towards a higher education (HE) qualification. However, both the Open University and CACHE offer STA qualifications that are national and externally awarded, with high standards of external monitoring and quality control. Some universities offer higher education qualifications, such as Certificates or Diplomas of Higher Education, specifically for teaching assistants. These are often developed and delivered in partnership with LEAs.

Awarding Bodies

ABC
Duxbury Park
Duxbury Hall Road
Chorley
Lancashire
PR7 4AT
tel: 01257 241428
e-mail: abc@centra.org.uk
www.abcawards.co.uk

City and Guilds
1 Giltspur Street
London
EC1A 9DD
tel: 020 7294 2800
e-mail: enquiry@city-and-
guilds.co.uk
www.city-and-guilds.co.uk

Council for Awards in Children's Care and Education (CACHE)
8 Chequer Street
St Albans
Herts
AL1 3XZ
tel: 01727 847636
e-mail: info@cache.org.uk
www.cache.org.uk

Edexcel Foundation
Stewart House
32 Russell Square
London
WC1B 5DN
tel: 0870 240 9800
e-mail: enquiries@edexcel.org.uk
www.edexcel.org.uk

NCFE
Citygate
St James Boulevard
Newcastle Upon Tyne
NE1 4JE
tel: 0191 239 8000
e-mail: info@ncfe.org.uk
www.ncfe.org.uk

NOCN
University of Derby
Kedleston Road
Derby
DE22 1GB
tel: 01332 622712
e-mail: nocn@derby.ac.uk
www.nocn.ac.uk

Oxford Cambridge and RSA Examinations (OCR)
Westwood Way
Coventry
CV4 8JQ
tel: 024 7647 0033
e-mail: cib@ocr.org.uk
www.ocr.org.uk

The Open University
PO Box 724
Milton Keynes
MK7 6ZS
tel: 01908 653231
e-mail: general-enquiries@
    open.ac.uk
www.open.ac.uk

Other useful contacts

Department for Education and Skills
Teaching Assistants Team
Area 6B
Sanctuary Buildings
Great Smith Street
London
SW1P 3BT
tel: 020 7925 5907
e-mail: assistants.teaching@
    dfes.gsi.gov.uk
www.teachernet.gov.uk

Employers' Organisation for Local Government
Layden House
76-86 Turnmill Street
London
EC1M 5LG
tel: 020 7296 6708
e-mail: lynne.butler@
    lg-employers.gov.uk
www.lgnto.gov.uk

Qualifications and Curriculum Authority
83 Piccadilly
London
W1J 8QA
tel: 020 7509 5556
e-mail: info@qca.org.uk
www.qca.org.uk

The Quality Assurance Agency for Higher Education
Southgate House
Southgate Street
Gloucester
GL1 1UB
tel: 01452 557000
e-mail: comms@qaa.ac.uk
www.qaa.ac.uk

The Teacher Training Agency
Portland House
Stag Place
London
SW1E 5TT
tel: 0845 6000 991 (for English speakers)
tel: 0845 6000 992 (for Welsh speakers)
e-mail: via the online advice form at www.canteach.gov.uk
www.canteach.gov.uk

A career structure for LSAs

Many LSAs are employed on temporary contracts, may not be paid if the child they support is absent and may lose their employment at short notice if the pupil progresses well, moves on or if their support is no longer justifiable in terms of local criteria and policies. It would be helpful to have guidelines for LEAs which enable ways of providing security of tenure for LSAs, with LSAs being employed on a permanent basis and linked to an incremental salary scale which reflects training, experience and special responsibilities.

Though there is, as yet, no national agreement on pay and conditions, the government, and the National Joint Council for Local Government Services (NJC) is currently considering the links between duties, skills, competencies and grading for support staff with a view to establishing a better-defined career path for all assistants.

Some final comments

As we move towards a recognition and formalising of the positive contribution of learning support assistants, it is interesting to reflect on how far we have come in using assistance in our schools.

The job of a classroom assistant has changed significantly over the last 15 years. The negative concept of a 'non-teaching assistant' employed to 'mix glazes, back books, clean paintpots and clear up messes' (to quote from a real job description of 1983) has gradually become obsolete. This idea of an assistant as a general dogsbody was replaced by the notion of an assistant as an extra pair of hands, a seemingly more positive concept but one which by implication suggested a 'reactive automaton' – not recognising that there is a thinking brain making the hands work!

In the last ten years, however, the potential of assistants who are, in the main, employed to support children who need learning support has been increasingly recognised. Schools are beginning to address the issues of support and training and the result is a more effective use of assistance and a much healthier concept of the role reflected now in the job title of learning support assistant.

The next few years will see the role more clearly described and there will continue to be improvements in both training opportunities and career structure. The framework for support and training, steered by the Department for Education and Employment, will provide consistency and ensure that high-quality training is accessible for all learning support assistants.

The happiest assistants are those who are valued by their colleagues in school and who are clear about their roles and responsibilities. In this handbook I have tried to suggest ways of working together in schools which will lead to a greater understanding of the role of a learning support assistant. I hope that it will encourage teachers and assistants to look together at how best to support each other and how best to support the pupils with whom they work.

Head teachers and SENCOs who employ assistants have a direct influence on and responsibility for the quality of their experience in school. I hope this book encourages managers to think carefully and creatively about how they manage this valuable resource and about the need for clear policy and procedures.

Above all, I hope I have given practical advice and reassurance to assistants which will enable them to be clearer about their roles and responsibilities and help them to work more confidently in supporting children, teachers and schools.

A job description suggestion for a learning support assistant

This job description is for an LSA working in a mainstream school. Specific adaptations would be necessary for assistants working in special schools.

JOB TITLE: **Learning Support Assistant**

POST HOLDER:

GRADE:

RESPONSIBLE TO: Head teacher/Class teacher/SENCO

RECEIVES INSTRUCTIONS FROM: Head teacher/Class teacher/SENCO

PURPOSE OF JOB: To assist in the support and inclusion of children with special educational needs.

JOB DUTIES:

A. Supporting the pupil

1. To develop a knowledge of a range of learning support needs and to develop an understanding of the specific needs of the child/ren to be supported.
2. Taking into account the learning support involved, to aid the child/ren to learn as effectively as possible both in group situations and on his/her own by, for example:
   – clarifying and explaining instructions;
   – ensuring the child is able to use equipment and materials provided;
   – motivating and encouraging the child as required;
   – assisting in weaker areas, e.g. language, behaviour, reading, spelling, handwriting/presentation etc;
   – helping pupils to concentrate on and finish work set;

– meeting physical needs as required whilst encouraging independence;
– liaising with class teacher and SENCO about individual education plans (IEPs);
– developing appropriate resources to support the child/ren.

3. To establish a supportive relationship with the child/ren concerned.
4. To encourage acceptance and inclusion of the child with special needs.
5. To develop methods of promoting/reinforcing the child's self-esteem.

B. Supporting the teacher

1. To assist, with class teacher (and other professionals as appropriate), in the development of a suitable programme of support (IEPs) for child/ren who need learning support.
2. In conjunction with the class teacher and/or other professionals to develop a system of recording the child's progress.
3. To contribute to the maintenance of child/ren's progress records.
4. To participate in the evaluation of the support programme.
5. To provide regular feedback about the child/ren to the teacher.

C. Supporting the curriculum

1. To develop a knowledge of the curriculum which the pupils are expected to follow.
2. To understand the National Strategies and their implications for pupils who require additional support.
3. To develop skills to adapt subject-based activities and resources to meet the needs of the pupil (in conjunction with the teacher).

D. Supporting the school

1. Where appropriate, to develop a relationship to foster links between home and school.
2. To liaise, advise and consult with other members of the team supporting the child/ren when asked to do so.
3. To contribute to reviews of children's progress, as appropriate.
4. To attend relevant in-service training.
5. To be aware of school procedures.
6. To be aware of confidential issues linked to home/pupil/teacher/school work and to keep confidences appropriately.

Any other tasks as directed by head teacher which fall within the purview of the post.

The roles of supporting professionals

During the course of your work in school, it is likely that you will come across one or more of the following professionals:

Physiotherapists

The physiotherapist identifies a child's main physical problems and devises a programme of treatment to overcome them. This may include: exercises, the use of splints or other aids, and advice on seating and general classroom handling.

Occupational therapists

The occupational therapist (OT) works with children who have difficulties with gross and fine motor coordination and/or perceptual problems. The OT is concerned with a child's functional independence in all daily activities from dressing to handwriting and special equipment is recommended where appropriate. OTs also work in child guidance services and can help with complex emotional and psychological needs.

Speech and language therapists

Speech and language therapists work with children who may have a wide range of disorders affecting their understanding and use of speech and/or language. They will assess the child's progress and provide a programme of activities aimed at developing listening skills, use of speech sounds, development of sentence structure etc.

Educational psychologists

Educational psychologists visit all schools on a regular basis in order to support children and the adults who work with them. They are called on to help and advise on a variety of educational problems. They may also devise programmes and carry out individual assessments. In addition, they are involved in assessment carried out under the 1981 Education Act, which may lead to a statement of special educational needs. They also work with schools to develop policies and practices, e.g. behaviour management.

Teacher advisers

As the title suggests, teacher advisers give advice to class teachers on specific issues. In addition, they may teach or assess individual children. Each teacher is usually a specialist in a specific area, e.g. learning difficulties, hearing impairment, physical disability, visual impairment etc.

SEN inspectors

Most local educational authorities have an inspector for special educational needs, who will advise schools on a range of SEN issues.

School medical officers (community paediatricians)

School medical officers are doctors who visit schools on a regular basis in order to see all children at certain stages in their school lives, and particular children as the need arises. They are able to provide diagnosis and to give advice about the medical implications of certain conditions.

APPENDIX C

Glossary of abbreviations

You will come across a considerable number of abbreviations in the course of your work. Here are some of the more common ones:

A Level	Advanced Level
ADD	Attention Deficit Disorder
AD/HD	Attention Deficit / Hyperactivity Disorder
AFASIC	Association for all Speech Impaired Children
AIDS	Acquired Immune Deficiency Syndrome
AR	Annual Review
AS	Advanced Supplementary Level
ASD	Autistic Spectrum Disorders
AT	Attainment Targets
BSS	Behaviour Support Service
CDT	Craft, Design and Technology
CEO	County Education Officer / Chief Education Officer
CF	Cystic Fibrosis
CMO	Clinical Medical Officer
CP	Cerebral Palsy
DART	Directed Activity Related to Text
DfES	Department for Education and Skills
EAL	English as an additional language
EBD	Emotional and Behavioural Difficulties
Ed Psych/EP	Educational Psychologist
EWO	Education Welfare Officer
GCSE	General Certificate of Secondary Education
GM	Grant Maintained
GNVQ	General National Vocational Qualification
HI	Hearing Impairment
HIV	Human Immunodeficiency Virus
HOF	Head of Faculty
HOY	Head of Year
ICT	Information and Communication Technology
IEP	Individual Education Plan
INSET	In-Service Training
LEA	Local Education Authority
LMS	Local Management of Schools
LSA	Learning Support Assistant

MDA	Multi-Disciplinary Assessment
ME	Myalgic Encephalomyelitis (Chronic Fatigue Syndrome)
MFL	Modern Foreign Languages
MLD	Moderate Learning Difficulties
MO	Medical Officer
MS	Multiple Sclerosis
NLS	National Literacy Strategy
NNS	National Numeracy Strategy
NVQ	National Vocational Qualification
OFSTED	Office for Standards in Education
OHP	Overhead Projector
OT	Occupational therapist
PIP	Progression in Phonics
PMLD	Profound and Multiple Learning Difficulties
PSHE	Personal Social and Health Education
PTA	Parent Teacher Association
RSA	Royal Society of Arts
SALT	Speech and Language Therapist
SDP	School Development Plan
SEN	Special Educational Needs
SENCO	Special Educational Needs coordinator
SLD	Severe Learning Difficulties
SMT	Senior Management Team
SNA	Special Needs Assistant
SpLD	Specific Learning Difficulties
TEC	Training and Enterprise Council
TES	Times Educational Supplement
VC	Voluntary Controlled
VI	Visual Impairment

References

Ainscow, M. and Tweddle, D. A. (1988) *Encouraging Classroom Success*. London: David Fulton Publishers.

Audit Commission/HMI (1992) *Getting in on the Act. A Management Handbook for Schools and LEAs*. London: HMSO.

Audit Commission/HMI (1992) *Getting the Act Together*. London: HMSO.

Balshaw, M. H. (1991) *Help in the Classroom*. London: David Fulton Publishers.

Bennett, A. (1985) *Meeting the Integration Needs of Partially Hearing Unit Pupils*. A.E.P. Journal, Vol. 6 No. 5. – Supplement.

Blind and Partially Sighted Children in Britain. The R.N.I.B. Survey, Vol. 12 London: HMSO.

Code of Practice on the identification and assessment of special educational needs. (1994) DfEE and Welsh Office.

Code of Practice in Special Educational Needs. (2001) DfES publications.

Cooper, P. and Ideus, K. (1996) *Attention Deficit/Hyperactivity Disorder – A Practical Guide for Teachers*. London: David Fulton Publishers.

Daines, B., Fleming, P. and Miller, C. (1996) *Spotlight on Special Educational Needs – Speech and Language Difficulties*, NASEN.

Excellence for all Children – Meeting Special Educational Needs, Green Paper (1997) DfEE.

Fenton, M. (1992) *Working Together Towards Independence*. London: RADAR – the Royal Association for Disability and Rehabilitation.

Fletcher-Campbell, F. (1992) 'How Can We Use an Extra Pair of Hands?', *British Journal of Special Education*, **19** (4).

Formal Assessment Procedures: Guidance for Parents, Hampshire Education Authority.

Fox, G. and Halliwell, M. (2000) *Supporting Literacy and Numeracy*. London: David Fulton Publishers.

Halliwell, M. (2003) *Supporting Children with Special Educational Needs*. London: David Fulton Publishers.

Lipsky, D. K. and Gartner, A. (1996) 'Inclusion, school restructuring and the remaking of American Society', *Harvard Educational Review*, **66** (4) 762–796.

Maines, B. and Robinson, G. *You Can – You Know You Can*, Course handbook to accompany workshops on the self-concept approach. Bristol: Lucky Duck Publishing.

Mallon, B. (1987) *An Introduction to Counselling Skills for Special Educational Needs*. Manchester University Press.

Meeting Special Needs Within the National Curriculum. (1989) Hampshire Education Authority.

Mitchell, G. (1997) *Practical Strategies for Individual Behaviour Difficulties.* London: David Fulton Publishers.

Principles of Good Practice – A Tool for Self-evaluation. (1992) Guidelines produced by the Hampshire Inspection and Advisory Support Service, Hampshire Education Authority.

Rieser, R. (1994) *Developing A Whole School Approach to Inclusion.* Available from Disability Equality in Education, 78 Mildmay Grove, London N1 4PJ.

Ripley, K., Daines, B. and Barrett, J. (1997) *Dyspraxia – A Guide for Teachers and Parents.* David Fulton Publishers.

Special Educational Needs (1978) Report of the Committee of Handicapped Children and Young People, HMSO (The Warnock report).